George Sachs PsyD
235 West 76th Street, 1B
New York, NY 10023

Sachscenter.com

Helping Your Husband with ADD/ADHD
George Sachs PsyD
ISBN 978-0996950718

Helping Your Husband with ADHD

Supportive Solutions for Adult ADD/ADHD

By George Sachs PsyD
& Timothy Norman LCSW

Contents

Why I Wrote This Book

"Jennifer" (not her real name) had reached the end of her patience. Tissues in hand, her tears flowed for what seemed like an eternity, as I listened to her recount the years of frustration she had endured at the hands of my client, who also happened to be her husband.

Was Jennifer's tale the plight of a battered woman seeking an escape from an unending cycle of violence at the mercy of an abusive husband? No. Thankfully, by her own account, Jennifer's husband never rose a hand against her in anger. In fact, he could be charming, exciting, and fun to be with. But he could also be irresponsible, lazy, inattentive and clueless regarding his role as a companion, husband, and father. His antics had led them to the brink of bankruptcy several times, leaving Jennifer holding the bag in terms of making an income and keeping her family afloat financially.

When her husband quit his umpteenth job after just four days, Jennifer hit bottom. She had no more emotional or physical energy to "keep up the charade," as she referred to what her marriage had become. Now she was in my office, tears flowing, asking – actually begging – for me to cure her husband or help her summon up the courage to leave him.

That's when the light bulb went off in my head. As a professional therapist, I had been trained to help the client in front of me deal with his or her problems. In Jennifer's case, I had been working with her husband first to encourage him to come to terms with his ADD/ADHD and then to work on strategies to mitigate some of the more damaging aspects of this disorder.

Although Jennifer was not the first wife to come to me with complaints about her husband's ADD/ADHD, this time was different. In the past my approach had been to help the wives develop strategies to deal with the daily stress that came with their situation.

Now, as I listened to Jennifer's story and watched her tears, I realized that I had been missing a key piece of the puzzle. Jennifer did not need me to help her manage her stress. Sure, I could give her some pointers on self-care and setting boundaries, but those were only band-aids. Instead, what Jennifer needed was a guidebook , a set of instructions to help her understand the ins and outs of ADD/ADHD from the point of view of the wife. She needed to get inside her husband's brain, hear from women who were fighting the same struggle, and learn what steps she could put into practice to help her husband manage the most debilitating aspects of ADD/ADHD as they affected not only his life, but hers as well.

Think about it this way: If Jennifer's husband suffered from diabetes, she would need to know a lot more than just how to make herself feel better about her situation. She would need to know the signs and symptoms of the disease as well as how to intervene to help her husband maintain his sugar equilibrium. The same holds true for ADD/ADHD.

As I came to this conclusion, it took all the effort I could muster not to interrupt Jennifer's need to unload and release her emotions. However, when the moment was right, I let her in on my thinking.

"Jennifer, I have an admission to make," I said, searching for the words that I hoped would set us both on an exciting new course of action. "You don't need sympathy, empathy, or even a listening ear. You need instructions!"

I went on to explain that ADD/ADHD is not just an excuse for selfish and inconsiderate behavior. It's an actual neurological disorder, similar in certain ways to other physical disorders that people might have. The goal in living with someone with ADD/ADHD is not simply to figure out ways to tolerate the situation, but to know what can and should be done to relieve the underlying symptoms. Instead of being a victim of her husband's behavior, Jennifer needed to become an active partner in helping him manage his condition.

Much has been written on managing the symptoms of ADD/ADHD, but these books were almost always directed at the client himself, as if it was up to the person with ADD/ADHD alone to solve his problems and get on with life. Yes, there were chat groups and forums where wives could air their complaints, but very few resources existed that gave wives tools to help their husbands deal with their challenges.

This book is an attempt to do just that: to bring together in one place a host of information to help wives not only understand their husband's condition, but also to empower them to steer their relationship in a healthier direction.

Since coming to this new understanding, I, along with my colleagues at the Sachs Center, have been able to help women gain a new understanding of ADD/ADHD and how they can transform their marriages from a living nightmare into a much more peaceful and harmonious one. As we wrote this book, we reached out to scores of men and women across the country to learn from their experiences. If you have picked up this book, then we both already know you need help. The good news is that you are not alone.

My sincere hope is that these pages will provide you with the information you need to begin your journey to a healthier and happier life, one that allows you to enjoy the excitement and creativity that first attracted you to your husband without falling victim to the excesses associated with his ADD/ADHD.

George Sachs Psy.D.

Introduction

He's restless. He's jumpy. He's impatient, impulsive, and chronically late! He simply refuses to get organized and puts off everything—and I mean everything—until the last minute.

Is this the guy you married? What the heck happened to him? Was he always this way? Or is it all in your head? More importantly, is there anything you can do to fix it, or do you have to suffer with his atrocious habits for the rest of your life?

If you are the wife of a man with ADD/ADHD this may have struck a painful chord, and for good reason. Beyond the daily difficulties of being on the receiving end of ADD/ADHD, your plight is often ignored by therapists and other professionals. Yes, many books and articles have been written describing the challenges of people with ADD/ADHD, but few focus on those who suffer the most from this condition – namely, their partners. This book is an attempt to do just that; to offer solid education and practical tips to help you deal with the daily frustrations of living with someone who has ADD/ADHD.

One note for the reader: While we embrace and encourage all healthy relationships, in order to facilitate easier reading and understanding, we will be using the term "wife" and "husband" throughout this book. We chose these words, as opposed to "partner," to zero in on the problem we see in our practice of married women dealing with their ADD/ADHD husbands. No offense is intended to those who are not married, or who live with a same sex partner. We hope this book is equally helpful to all individuals (single, straight, gay) living with a significant other who has ADD/ADHD.

As a starting point, let's review some important labels and terms that will be used throughout this book. This will help avoid confusion as you learn not only about the various difficulties associated with ADD/ADHD, but also how to improve your daily life and relationship with your partner.

- ADHD – Attention Deficit Hyperactive Disorder (the clinical term)
- ADD – Attention Deficit Disorder (the colloquial term)

While ADHD is the proper clinical term, many adults don't exhibit the "H" (for hyperactivity). This led in the last two decades to the abbreviated form, ADD. In practical terms, this means is that many adults are not hyperactive in the manner as we imagine young children to be, yet they still manifest symptoms of impulsivity, restlessness and a strong feeling of being constantly on the go or "driven by a motor." While diagnostically incorrect, the term ADD has become mainstream in our society.

EFDD, or Executive Functioning Deficit Disorder, has only recently been proposed as an updated and more accurate description of this disorder. ADD/ADHD expert Dr. Russell Barkley has suggested that ADD/ADHD is really a problem with executive functioning, which includes not just focus, but also organization, time management, prioritization, impulsivity, emotional regulation and more.

For the purposes of this book, unless specifically noted, we will use the term ADD/ADHD, which effectively covers most of the challenges wives face when dealing with their husbands in this regard.

It is also important to remember that not all ADD/ADHD is created equal. In other words, some people have very mild symptoms of ADD/ADHD that go unnoticed for years, while others have very severe challenges that have significantly affected their daily lives since childhood. Educating yourself about your husband's ADD/ADHD is a compassionate act. Give yourself credit for caring enough about yourself, your husband, and your marriage to take time out of your day to improve both of your lives. The answers to our problems are not always easy. But with a little work, and a lot of love, you have the power to change your life—and his.

PART 1

WHAT IS ADD/ADHD?

[1]

A Different Brain

According to the *Wall Street Journal*, some 10 million American adults suffer from ADD/ADHD. Even worse, less than 25 percent of these individuals know they even have it (but their wives probably do!).

Typically, the symptoms of ADD/ADHD first show themselves in childhood. However, as we mentioned, many, if not most, never receive a diagnosis or the help they need. What happens when a hyperactive, distracted, or inattentive child manages to get through adolescence and into adulthood without a diagnosis?

Until recently—nothing.

Historically, the medical establishment has focused on ADD/ADHD as a childhood disease. It was not until the 1980s that psychologists even began to entertain the idea that the disorder could progress well into adulthood. Before this time, symptoms of ADD/ADHD may have been integrated into alternative diagnoses including OCD, anxiety disorders, or even bipolar disorder or schizophrenia. Such mislabeling could be highly problematic for the person affected and his family and friends.

As adults, those with ADD/ADHD may appear to be scattered, unfocused, unreliable, unpredictable, or simply annoying to co-workers, spouses, and pretty much anyone else who has to deal with them. They may have difficulty finding or holding down a job, their personal relationships may suffer, or they may just feel generally scattered and unhappy. These problems are compounded by years of underachievement, feelings of failure, depression, and low self-esteem.

Left untreated, men with ADD/ADHD are unlikely to do much of anything positive to reduce their symptoms on their own. Sure, they may self-medicate with alcohol or other substances, but this only magnifies the problem. The result of untreated ADD/ADHD can mean years of anger, frustration, and loneliness for their wives, who are often left to their own devices in terms of keeping their families from descending into chaos.

Lisa H., is an IT help-desk consultant with a major manufacturer in the Midwest. She described the conflicting emotions she wrestles with regarding her ADD/ADHD husband.

Let me start off by saying that I love my husband. I really do. Do I want to kill him sometimes? Oh my God, yes! Don't get me wrong; he's an incredibly loving, protective, and loyal husband and father. But, sometimes I feel like I have three children instead of two. It's not that he isn't a good provider, or that he's an absentee parent—I mean he's not physically absent, but mentally, sometimes I wonder.

Does this mean that every insensitive, easily distracted husband suffers from ADD/ADHD? Of course not. It's about the degree to which his issues negatively affect his life, career, and family. The greater the impairment in functioning, the higher the probability that he meets criteria for a diagnosis of ADD/ADHD.

Adult ADD/ADHD is a newly understood psychological disorder, which means it is not always easy to obtain an accurate diagnosis. As previously stated, some of the symptoms associated with ADD/ADHD are also seen in patients with anxiety or other psychological disorders. The challenge for psychologists and psychiatrists is to determine the primary disorder that needs to be treated. Are your husband's challenges related to his anxiety, ADD/ADHD, depression, or all three?

If you are like most wives of men with ADD/ADHD, you may have asked yourself, "Is my husband annoying because he likes to drive me crazy or does he really suffer from an identifiable problem?" Until recently, therapists may have tried to treat the symptoms without recognizing that their adult patient also suffers from ADD/ADHD. If you can be married to someone for over 20 years and still miss it, then someone who has only had a few sessions with him may not notice it, either.

To top it off, some women prefer men with ADD/ADHD. They may not see it as a problem. Especially in the early stages of a relationship, men with ADD/ADHD are often quick, smart and creative. They possess great charisma, and can be brilliant in the areas that capture their interest. Some of these men achieve tremendous success, despite having to cope with the difficulties presented by ADD/ADHD. When an individual suffers from a particular problem for a long time, he often comes up with creative and functional ways to cope with it.

For example, according to a report in the *Wall Street Journal,* David Neeleman, the founder of JetBlue Airways, and Paul Orfalea, founder of Kinkos, have stated that their ADD/ADHD helped them come up with innovative ideas for their corporations, despite their poor academic history. When it comes down to it, there are two kinds of intelligence: book smarts and street smarts. Although men with ADD/ADHD may lack the skills to turn in perfect papers or perform on standardized tests, their fast-moving brains and creativity may have helped them develop into successful "out-of-the-box" thinkers who could transform whole industries.

Nevertheless, these types of success stories are rare exceptions. The vast majority of wives can testify to the fact that living with an ADD/ADHD man is a daily struggle, full of large and small frustrations that only add to an already stressful life. (But if you are reading this book, you already know this.)

So what do we know about ADD/ADHD in adults? Let's start with what ADD/ADHD *is not.* ADD/ADHD is not the result of bad parenting, childhood trauma, or any environmental factors. Instead it is a disorder in brain function. Genetics also play a large role in the development of ADD/ADHD. Eight out of ten people diagnosed with ADD/ADHD have at least one parent with the disorder. This is also important information if you are wondering if your child has ADD/ADHD. Chances are one of them might.

More specifically, ADD/ADHD stems from miscommunication between different parts of the brain. This disconnect seems to be exacerbated by an imbalance in neurotransmitters, the chemical messengers that relay signals within the brain. This is particularly evident in the frontal cortex, which controls planning, impulse control and other "executive functions."

In young children, particularly boys, ADD/ADHD can manifest as constant motion. That's the reason for the "H" in ADHD: it stands for "hyperactive." The constant need for movement does not just mean that the motor never stops running. It makes many vital tasks—such as sitting still and learning in school (or, later in life, listening to one's spouse)—much more difficult. Before anything seems to start, the train has already left the station.

Psychologists and parents also face the challenge of trying to determine the difference between ADD/ADHD symptoms and normal "kid stuff." With boys, ADD/ADHD often goes undiagnosed for years, be-cause parents assume the symptoms are just "boys will be boys," a passing phase, or due to growth spurts. By the time it becomes clear that the problems are more pronounced, many years have already passed.

With adult men, the symptoms of ADD/ADHD manifest themselves in a different manner. The hyperactivity common to pediatric ADD/ADHD now appear as impulsivity, procrastination and organiza-tional deficits. Certain struggles, like the ability to set priorities or focus on the task at hand, start to interfere with normal functioning in much more detrimental ways. Managing time and money also pose huge chal-lenges for ADD/ADHD men—and their wives, who must swoop in to pick up the pieces. Nevertheless, pinning such life-skill challenges on ADD/ADHD is not always so easy. How does a wife know when she's dealing with a full-blown case of ADD/ADHD?

Dr. Ivan K. Goldberg is a psychiatrist in New York City who co-developed a commonly used test to screen for ADD/ADHD. Assigning a diagnosis, he pointed out, depends on the "amount and intensity" of the dysfunction. As we have pointed out, Dr. Goldberg regards ADD/ADHD as "disturbance of the executive functions of the brain. It's the inability to plan things, to initiate them at the appropriate time, not to skip any of the steps, and to terminate them at the appropriate time. An awful lot of these people are very bright, but they can't keep it to-gether, they keep screwing things up."

Rob C., 38, works for a social service agency in New York City. As someone with ADD/ADHD, Rob identifies with Dr. Goldberg's worlds. "There's a huge incidence of depression, because you are continually failing in the eyes of others, not reaching your potential," he said. "Peo-ple recognize you are smart, and you can't find your niche." The sense of failure may kick in at a particular point in an ADD/ADHD man's ca-reer, or it may follow them through a series of life transitions, adding a not-so-silent commentary to the soundtrack of their lives. Many times, men with ADD/ADHD have developed coping mechanisms that help them advance fairly far. They may find a good job, or get into law school, or get married -- only to hit a wall when their coping mechanisms break down.

Dr. Peter Jaksa, who suffers from ADD/ADHD himself, works as a clinical psychologist in Chicago. He vividly remembers when his ADD/ADHD began to get the better of him, long after graduate school when he was already in practice, working with underachieving kids. "Once you know what it is, things make sense that didn't make sense previously," he said. As an example, he vividly recalled his pattern of writing every college paper the night before it was due, with a six-pack of Mountain Dew and a box of Red Bull at his side.

Ultimately, even when men with ADD/ADHD enjoy professional success—and many do not—it comes with a cost. Living life constantly behind the eight-ball takes a toll in terms of wasted time, choppy family life, and frayed nerves for everyone involved.

"If your husband has ADD/ADHD, his level of distraction and disorganization interferes with the basics of his life, causing a major *impairment*," Dr. Jaksa said. "Impairment is the magic word. Everyone gets distracted. Who's not late occasionally? But if you are chronically late, you lose your job and maybe your friends as well."

John K., a writer currently living Miami, at first tried to confine his messy habits to his bedroom, figuring that he could laugh it off as one of the perks of being single. It was not long before the mess spread throughout his entire house. Bills went unpaid. Projects lay unfinished. Deadlines came and went. At one point, he found himself involved in a string of minor car accidents that he could never explain. At age 35, he could no longer pass off these occurrences as a case of extended adolescence. Certainly, the women in his life no longer felt like giving him a pass. Instead, he felt as if his life was spiraling out of control.

It wasn't that I didn't want to get my life in order. I just wasn't capable of doing it. There's a big difference between not doing something because you don't want to and not doing something because, for some reason, you simply can't.

It's not always just ADD/ADHD that affects relationships, but the concurrent disorders often associated with it. In his book, *Driven to Distraction,* Dr. Edward Hallowell calls attention to a number of disorders that may accompany ADD/ADHD. These include depression, anxiety, agitation or mania, substance abuse, Conduct Disorder, Oppositional Disorder, Borderline Personality features, Obsessive-Compulsive Disorder, and/or learning disorders.

ADD/ADHD has even been linked to criminal behavior. A study of prisoners in Norrtälje Prison in Sweden estimated that four out of ten of the inmates there had ADD/ADHD, with only 6.6 percent receiving an early childhood diagnosis of the disorder. All subjects reported substance abuse, and mood and anxiety disorders were present in half of the subjects.

In 2009, researchers at the Adult Attention Deficit Disorder Center of Maryland at Johns Hopkins University looked at studies done between 1998 and 2008 on the prevalence, persistence, and consequences of ADD/AHDH in adults. They also looked at the relationship between adult ADD/ADHD and mood disorders. Results showed that most children with ADD/ADHD had symptoms that persisted into adulthood. When left untreated, these behaviors adversely affect school and work achievements, diminish self-esteem, damage interpersonal relationships, and significantly reduce quality of life for adults.

Before we move on to a more detailed exploration of the various ways in which ADD/ADHD can affect your relationship and what you can do about it, let's take a moment to review the top ten ways in which

ADD/ADHD manifests itself in adult men. The following list of problems is described in more detail at WebMD.com. If you see five or more of these symptoms leading to impaired functioning, you may want to encourage your husband to obtain a full diagnosis from a competent professional.

- Difficulty Getting Organized
- Reckless Driving and/or Traffic Accidents
- Marital Trouble
- Extremely Distractible
- Poor Listening Skills
- Restlessness, Trouble Relaxing
- Inability to Start Tasks
- Chronic Lateness
- Frequent Angry Outbursts

[2]

An Accurate Diagnosis

The Diagnostic and Statistical Manual (DSM) for the American Psychological Association (APA) asserts that your husband may have ADD/ADHD if he has experienced six or more of the following symptoms regularly for at least the past six months:

Inattention:
- Often fails to give close attention to details or makes careless mistakes
- Difficulty sustaining attention
- Appears as though he is not listening when spoken to
- Fails to follow through with instructions or tasks (not as a result of purposeful rebellion)
- Difficulty getting or staying organized
- Avoids, dislikes or hesitates to engage in tasks that require sustained attention
- Often loses or misplaces things

- Is easily distracted
- Frequent forgetfulness

Hyperactivity:
- Frequent fidgeting or squirming
- Often getting up from their his seat at inappropriate times
- Excessive physical activity or self-reported feelings of restlessness
- Difficulty engaging in leisure activities quietly
- Appears to be driven by an internal motor that seems to never stop running

These symptoms must have been present in the individual before the age of twelve. They must also be present in two or more settings (e.g., work and home) and the individual must be experiencing significant impairment in his or her ability to function at a developmentally appropriate level. Individuals who demonstrate at least six of the symptoms for both inattention AND hyperactivity qualify for the diagnosis of ADD/ADHD.

Dr. Edward Hallowell's book, *Driven to Distraction*, describes a few other telltale signs that can further clarify whether the individual might have ADD/ADHD. However, these signs serve as just that—signs. Having a few of these symptoms might be a problem, but it does not necessarily mean that the individual has the real disorder.

According to Dr. Hallowell, anyone exhibiting at least 12 of the following characteristics since childhood, where the characteristics are not associated with any other psychological or medical condition, should consider being evaluated for ADD/ADHD:

- A persistent sense of underachievement, of not meeting one's goals (regardless of how much one has actually accomplished)
- Difficulty getting and/or staying organized
- Chronic procrastination or trouble initiating tasks
- Tendency to take on many projects simultaneously with trouble following through
- Lack of a verbal "filter"; the tendency to say what comes to mind without necessarily considering the timing or appropriateness of the remark
- Frequently in search of increasing levels of stimulation
- An intolerance of boredom
- Easily distractible; trouble focusing attention, tendency to tune out or drift away in the middle of a page or conversation, often coupled with an inability to focus at times
- Often creative, intuitive, highly intelligent, but slightly eccentric
- Lack of conformity and/or following "proper" procedure when pursuing goals
- Impatience; low tolerance for frustration
- Impulsivity, either verbally or in action (i.e., impulsively spending money or being hot tempered)
- Frequently changing plans, enacting new schemes or career plans
- A persistent tendency to worry needlessly; scanning the horizon looking for something to worry about, alternating with attention to or disregard for actual dangers
- A sense of insecurity
- Mood swings, especially when not currently engaged with a person or project
- Physical or cognitive restlessness

- A tendency toward addictive behavior
- Chronic problems with self-esteem
- Inaccurate self-observation; lack of personal insight
- Family history of ADD/ADHD, manic-depressive illness, depression, substance abuse, or other disorders of impulse control or mood

Many of these signs overlap with the DSM diagnostic criteria. However, there are others that do not. Some of them may be more indicative of another mental illness, so it is important to identify the primary problem. According to a 2007 study in Primary Care: Clinics in Office Practice, childhood ADD/ADHD symptoms often evolve into the following adult symptoms:

- Procrastination
- Indecision; difficulty recalling and organizing details required for a task
- Poor time management; losing track of time
- Avoiding tasks or jobs that require sustained attention
- Trouble initiating tasks
- Difficulty completing and following through on tasks
- Seeming inability to multitask
- Difficulty shifting attention from one task to another

Although a diagnosis of ADD/ADHD may initially be shocking to you and your family, you can breathe a sigh of relief, knowing you finally have a medical explanation for your husband's difficult behavior. What's more, you can start to take steps to help manage the disorder and improve both your lives.

In the meantime, remember that a diagnosis of ADD/ADHD does not imply low intelligence. You don't have to speak louder or more slowly for your husband to understand you. In fact, most people with ADD/ADHD are highly intelligent. It's just that their intelligence gets tangled up inside their brain and needs to be smoothed out in order for them to function optimally.

Many psychological conditions can be detected by a blood test or brain scan. Some disorders are so distinct that there can be only one explanation for them. Unfortunately, this is not the case with ADD/ADHD. In fact, it can be difficult to make a definitive diagnosis for this disorder, because there is no single test with which to confidently diagnose the disorder. Only a licensed and trained mental health professional can administer the current panel of evaluations to properly diagnose ADD/ADHD. Be wary of online quizzes claiming to diagnose ADD/ADHD quickly or for free. There is no quick diagnosis, just as there is no quick fix to treat it. Since diagnosis can be difficult, and carries a life-sentence, it is imperative that the testing be done carefully and completely. Invest the time and money necessary to get the correct diagnosis the first time, and work only with mental health professionals with whom you feel comfortable.

A qualified professional should conduct a series of evaluations to provide an official diagnosis. At the Sachs Center, we employ three different methods of testing to arrive at a diagnosis. This comprehensive three hour evaluation begins with a personal interview to review the client's medical and psychological history. Checklists are also employed that are tested and researched by universities. An example is the Adult ADHD Self-Report Scale-V1.1 (ASRS-V1.1). Second, the client completes a computer exercise to uncover deficits in visual and auditory attention span symptoms of ADD/ADHD. We use and recommend the IVA+Plus, created by BrainTrain (www.braintrain.com). The IVA+Plus, and other computer-based performance tests provide objective data regarding a person's ability to concentrate and to avoid making impulsive errors. Lastly, the client completes a battery of several short tests to assess working memory, processing speed, and executive functioning. While each test alone cannot assess for ADD/ADHD, together they provide a clearer picture of the individual's strengths and weaknesses and help the clinician come to an accurate diagnosis.

Some clinics recommend an expensive, eight-hour, neuropsychological assessment to determine a diagnosis of ADD/ADHD. This is generally not necessary unless there are other serious co-occurring mental health or neurological issues.

[3]

Self-Regulation Disorder

The traditional view that ADD/ADHD was simply a problem of attention and focus has changed in the last decade to include all areas of self-regulation. In fact, Dr. Russell Barkley of the Department of Psychiatry at the SUNY Upstate Medical University in Syracuse, NY, a leading researcher in ADHD, suggests that a better name for ADD/ADHD is "Self-Regulation Disorder."

A major difficulty for men with ADD/ADHD is the regulation of their emotions. They become easily irritated, annoyed, impatient, and prone to blowups and bouts of moodiness, which obviously can wreak havoc on a marriage. Barbara L., of New London, Connecticut, finds herself bridling at what she sees as her husband's complete lack of empathy for other people.

Someone dies—he will laugh. He also is highly defensive and always looking to argue. He likes it . . . I think he's comfortable being angry.

Monique, P., an event planner from Richmond, Virginia, also lacks an effective way of dealing with her husband's anger.

> *I'm often told I'm weak or too sensitive. He thinks I'm the enemy. Even when we try to talk something out, he can't control himself from being angry, mean, and blaming me. No matter how nice I try to speak and all the apologies I utter—to the point where I don't even know why I'm sorry—there is no stepping outside himself.*

She characterized the level of her miscommunication problems with her husband at "90 percent." Other wives of men with ADD/ADHD find they cannot get their husbands to discuss even simple household tasks without risking a fight.

> *If I want to talk about a household project like cleaning out the basement, he blows up that I'm always nagging him about stupid stuff. I've tried using less confrontational methods like emailing or texting him when I have a question for him or want to bounce an idea off him, but now he just screens all of my messages and ignores them. If I ask him if he got them, he'll come right out and tell me that he doesn't even always read them. When I express how I feel disrespected when he ignores my messages, he goes off like a time bomb.*
>
> *-- Cheryl B., Charlotte, North Carolina*

Barbara, Monique, Cheryl, and countless others in similar situations assume there is no hope for getting their husbands to change. However, recent research into ADD/ADHD and emotional regulation offers a new perspective that can help both partners create better coping strategies.

One of the questions plaguing therapists, researchers and scientists—as well as people with ADD/ADHD themselves—is determining the source of the problem. Are the emotional challenges faced by people with ADD/ADHD a disorder, or a more psycho-physiological regulatory issue? In other words, are the emotions of these men inappropriate and disconnected from actual events (i.e., bipolar disorder), or are their emotions appropriate, but totally out of proportion and poorly managed?

Recent research indicates that rather than stemming from a disorder, emotional regulation problems among the ADD/ADHD population grow out of a flaw in the person's executive functioning. Thus, the proposed new diagnostic name: Executive Function Deficit Disorder.

If Dr. Barkley, an advocate of this view, and other like-minded psychologists are successful, you may see a change in the acronym and diagnosis of ADD/ADHD within the next five or ten years. As new research is conducted, and the field of psychology advances, such changes in diagnoses will become more common. For now, it is helpful to look at ADD/ADHD through the lens of executive functioning, because those are the functions most inhibited by chemical imbalance and poor communication within the brain.

If the challenge is related to executive functioning, then the emotions experienced by men with ADD/ADHD are in fact normal. That's the good news. The bad news is that even normal emotions can leave a trail of destruction in their wake if their expression is left unregulated. A good teapot whistles when the water boils. A bad teapot is always boiling and therefore always whistling.

Dr. Barkley explains that for many people, getting reprimanded by a superior at work can cause a strong, even violent, emotional response. The difference between people with ADD/ADHD and others is in how they regulate themselves during that event. Most people know how to control their impulses and immediate reactions. This buys them a few seconds to think about a healthy response, and then respond appropriately. Men with ADD/ADHD are more likely to lash out, create a scene, and immediately express the intense emotions they are feeling. The emotions they feel are appropriate. The way they act on them is not.

One major reason for this lack of control, according to Dr. Barkley, has to do with the internal wiring of the ADD/ADHD brain. Someone with ADD/ADHD lacks a neurological control mechanism that exists between the frontal lobe of the brain—the Executive – and the much more primitive portions of our brain where the raw emotions reside.

The fact that the problem of emotional regulation centers on "wiring" offers hope to wives of men with ADD/ADHD. Research shows that couples can engage in a number of re-wiring strategies to help regulate the husband's emotional response.

Consider the following tips to improve self-regulation:

For Him: Learn impulse control. If your husband has the tendency to get angry at others, seemingly at the drop of a hat, or interrupt without permission, he can manage his impulses by learning to count to ten. Ask him to take some time BEFORE he responds to you to think over his decision. Instead of "acting out," encourage him to "breath out"— s-l-o-w-l-y. In fact, since his ADD/ADHD mind enjoys rapid change, the shift of attention to counting and breathing may help the impulse pass as quickly as it appeared.

Find an outlet for all that energy. One thing man with ADD/ADHD does not lack is nervous energy. Instead of allowing this excess to express itself inappropriately in emotional interactions, channel it into a hobby. In one case, a man who had struggled with ADD/ADHD his whole life became a mountain biking enthusiast. He eventually opened a bike shop and organized biking races and outings for his city. It worked wonders for his marriage, because he had an outlet for his energy.

Learn about triggers. By learning what physical triggers spark his unhealthy emotions, you can better understand WHEN an unregulated emotion may arise. For example: Does he lose it when talking with customer service reps on the phone? Or does waiting in line at the bank make him crazy? When we learn our triggers, we can avoid them. Maybe you can make the customer service calls and do the banking. Perhaps making dinner or doing the dishes are more soothing for him.

For You: Look to your actions. While it may be a chicken-and-egg question, some of your husband's rude, uncaring, and emotionally inappropriate behavior may not be completely off base. He may be responding to the way you react to his symptoms. Take a good look at your responses to his behavior. Substituting positive reinforcement for nagging may mitigate much of the tension in the household. Catch him "being good' and praise the hell of out him.

Don't assume you know your husband's motives. If your husband's actions stem from an inadequacy in his executive functioning skills, do not assume he is deliberately trying to hurt your feelings. If you feel hurt by something he said or did, call attention to it in as neutral a manner as possible. Tell him that his actions have had an impact, intended, or unintended.

Look for practical solutions. Transfer your emotional responses into the realm of practical logistics. For example, if you feel ignored, take that feeling and make a concrete response, such as scheduling a date night on the calendar, which addresses the issues. This will most likely be more effective than talking about your feelings and hoping he will respond the way you want him to. Direct the response you want by creating the practical solution.

Get him moving. Men with ADD/ADHD like to move, so sitting on the couch hashing out your feelings may make him feel trapped and penned in—which could lead to an unhelpful emotional reaction on his part. Suggest a walk outside. This will get him moving and minimize direct eye contact (often threatening to guys with ADD/ADHD).

For Both: Use humor and fun to defuse issues. Make up a lighthearted "miscommunication" song or phrase—or some similar strategy—that you can use when something he says or does rubs you the wrong way. One couple uses the word "ouch" to suggest something said or done landed the wrong way. Or simply agree that you will both learn to laugh at certain situations, and then correct them in a pleasant tension-free atmosphere.

[4]

Five Major Symptoms of ADD/ADHD

Is your garage full of thousands of dollars' worth of useless products that your ADD/ADHD husband bought while watching late-night info-mercials? Have you had to extricate yourself from one too many expensive impulse purchases that he locked you into when you weren't looking? Do you cringe every time your husband walks out of the house and heads to the mall, wondering what strange item will accompany your husband when he returns home?

If any of these situations brings up a knowing sense of dread, then you are already familiar with another challenge faced by the wives of ADD/ADHD husbands: lack of impulse control.

Impulsivity

To be sure, your husband's constant need for something new and exciting to focus on may not always extend to needlessly spending your hard-earned cash. The lack of impulse control exhibited by ADD/ADHD men extends to a number of areas, including how they act at work, with friends and in social situations. However, many wives fear their husband's lack of control in the financial realm more than anything else, because it leaves them feeling particularly vulnerable. Once the money is gone, it's gone.

Repeatedly, wives of ADD/ADHD men cringe at the memory of personal horror stories related to their husband's lack of impulse control with regard to money. Ann R. From Freehold, New Jersey, relates the following:

One day, my dear husband decided we needed a grand piano. I have no idea where he got this idea, but believe me, he had it all figured out. He was going to borrow half of the money from the bank, based on my parents co-signing the loan. The rest was going to go on the credit card. Thank heaven I was able to talk him out of it—this time. But this is the kind of thing I have to deal with constantly!

Marla W., who runs a consignment shop outside of Detroit, Michigan, did not escape so easily. Her ADD/ADHD husband bought a $35,000 minivan that turned out to be a complete lemon.

Others report even more harrowing experiences due to their husband's lack of impulse control. Lori N., a physician's assistant in Austin, Texas, tearfully recalled how her husband bought a three-bedroom house on an island—sight unseen. Getting out of the deal cost them thousands of dollars in legal fees.

Perhaps most heartbreakingly, Cheryl W., a homemaker living outside of Chicago, Illinois, woke up one day to discover that, on the "advice" of a salesman, her husband had purchased a laundromat. They lost more than $200,000 in the venture, which ultimately went bankrupt.

Beyond the anxiety and aggravation that comes from watching their ADD/ADHD husbands career through life, many wives are at a loss to explain why their husbands cannot simply control themselves.

It's one thing to have to pick up his dirty clothes all the time. I get it. He can't stop himself from dropping his socks. But how does this translate into spending hundreds or thousands of dollars on stuff we don't need?

--- Cindy A., New Haven, Connecticut

Decision-Making

Some research appears to draw a link between the lack of impulse control associated with ADD/ADHD and faulty problem-solving abilities. In other words, rather than giving into their impulses (which may in fact be the case), ADD/ADHD men fail to take their brains through the normal problem-solving steps other people employ as a matter of course. Their problem is not a lack of impulse control per se, but more a matter of giving up too early in the whole decision-making process.

Susan Young, PhD, a clinical psychologist at the Institute of Psychiatry in London, tackled this subject in a study published in *Neuropsychology*. The study required participants to solve a series of on-screen puzzles at varying levels of difficulty. Each progressive puzzle required an increasing number of moves on the part of the participants. One of the components tracked by Dr. Young and her team included the time lag between the appearance of the puzzle and a participant's first move. As the puzzles became more difficult, participants with ADD/ADHD failed to allocate additional time to planning. Instead, they plowed through the more difficult puzzles at the same pace they used on the easier ones. Predictably, their success rate declined as compared to a control group. According to Dr. Young, the ADD/ADHD group favored speed over accuracy, resulting in what she termed "ineffective, haphazard strategies."

Purchasing a big-ticket item requires complex problem-solving skills. Someone willing to put down thousands of dollars on a business venture without properly reviewing the different facets of the deal most likely skips any number of important decisions along the way. Instead, the need for resolution to the problem trumps cooler-headed logic—a classic challenge associated with ADD/ADHD.

While it is unwise to draw definitive conclusions from one study, the results of Dr. Young's research may offer hope to wives who wish to help their ADD/ADHD husbands conquer their lack of impulse control. Instead of trying to constrain her husband's spending habits, for example, a wife may achieve better results by working with her husband to improve his decision-making process. This helps address the problem closer to the source, rather than after the expression of the behavior. In other words, once a husband changes the way he solves problems, the problem of impulse control is less likely to wreak havoc on his bank account, jobs, friendships—and marriage.

Color-coding the decision-making process helps. The brain-child of Maltese physician, author, inventor, and consultant Eduardo de Bono, this strategy is known as "six-hat thinking," and is described in full detail in his book, *Six Thinking Hats.*

For men with ADD/ADHD, this system helps them avoid rash decisions by including a built-in method of changing perspectives. Instead of skipping the uncomfortable process of linear decision-making, six-hat thinking purposely requires a shift in focus. In brief, the technique assigns a color to six distinct methods of processing information:

White Hat: This style of thinking centers on the information or the "data" available at the moment. What are the observable facts that two different people could both agree on. This is the opportunity for the ADD/ADHD husband to quickly gain a sense of costs, benefits, and other relevant facts and figures. It also highlights any gaps in information that need to be filled in.

Black Hat: Like the bad guys in the cowboy movies, black-hat thinking focuses on the negative points of going with a certain decision. This is also important data to discern for men with ADD/ADHD, offering them a chance to act as their own devil's advocate.

Yellow Hat: On the other end of the spectrum, yellow-hat thinking focuses on the upside of the decision. It allows your husband to dream the dream, but since he will be changing focus momentarily, you do not have to worry that he will get locked in a "purchasing state of mind."

Red Hat: Driven by the fire of emotion, red-hat thinking zeroes in on gut reactions, intuition and unfiltered feelings surrounding a proposed course of action. This allows the man with ADD/ADHD to utilize their "gut" instincts. This can be faulty at times but is not to be overlooked.

Green Hat: Green means go, and in this case, it stands for creative thinking. Green-hat thinking focuses on ways to solve a problem. "If I decide to proceed, what possible consequences will emerge and what other decisions will need to be made?" This also fits well with the ADD/ADHD mindset, because it allows for free-thinking without limits.

Blue Hat: Blue hat thinking creates an overall process to this decision tree. If your husband agrees to the process of going through this process whenever he faces a major decision (e.g., buying a new car), then he is successfully employing blue-hat thinking.

Six-hat thinking fits well with the way ADD/ADHD men go about their routines. For example, when your husband sets out on a shopping trip, encourage him to carry six color-coded cards and flip through each card—at whatever speed he wishes—prior to making a final decision. The shift in focus may be sufficient to overrule the momentary desire to act on the buying impulse (or other impulses as well).

The six-hat strategy also helps improve communication habits. Instead of nagging or expressing concern, you and your husband can agree beforehand to simply do the six-hat dance. This will put a more enjoyable face on the issue and reduce tension all around.

Distractibility

Of all the symptoms exhibited by men with ADD/ADHD, their inability to deal with distractions may be the most frustrating for their wives. Ann S., a graduate student living outside Bethesda, Maryland, knows that the instant she starts talking to her ADD/ADHD husband, his "distraction clock" is already ticking.

Forget about trying to have a real discussion about how my day was, our relationship, or ANY topic that takes more than 60 seconds to complete. He completely loses focus and tunes me out. He'll fidget, play with the dog, switch the channels on the television. It's like our living room becomes an activity center for him. It's like living with a three-year-old in a 30-year-old's body.

Most men with ADD/ADHD know they suffer from an overabundance of distraction. In extreme cases, the slightest outside input takes them off track. If they go upstairs to find a book, for example, they may not return for a long time. The reason? They have just entered a whole new room, replete with "shiny new objects" to occupy their time. This inability to adequately filter their environment, discarding unwanted information or interests, has the power to throw off their daily lives, academic careers, jobs, and marriages.

Douglas Cootey is the author of the blog *The Splintered Mind*, which describes his experiences dealing with ADD/ADHD. In one particularly enlightening post, he recalls what it was like for him to sit for an exam during college. The difficulty in filtering unwanted distractions, he noted, is that "the foreground and background noise tend to switch places within my addled brain." He writes:

This is one reason I despised taking exams [during college]. When my mind grew accustomed to the quiet [of the testing room], the real fun began. The room filled with sniffles and coughs, like bird calls in an aviary. The sniffles evolved into snuffles, which were eventually replaced by pencil tapping. Seemingly harmless to those with normal brains, the gentle strikes of No. 2 pencils hammered my ADD/ADHD brain like blows in a steel foundry.

The notion that men with ADD/ADHD experience "all noise as equal" rings true with many wives, who watch in amazement and frustration as their husbands career through a life in a constant state of distraction. Sometimes it seems as if the only time frame that exists is "now." Everything begins but never finishes, whether it is a conversation, a project, an errand or any task.

Jenny K. is an emergency room nurse in Tulsa, Oklahoma. She is well acquainted with the frantic pace of events and the need to shift focus that makes up life in an emergency room. However, when it comes to her colleagues in the ER, they know how to stay on task. At home with her husband, it's a different story.

Ninety-five percent of our fights begin with me saying something like, 'Hey, did you get a chance to do X yet? But forget it. I literally feel like I am talking to a wall. He is simply not present. He will go off on an errand and leave me with the kids and disappear for hours and never come back with the original thing—and then he has to head out all over again. Or he will decide to start a new project instead of the one he's already started and leave me with the kids, and then he'll lose interest, and I'll catch him playing video games or something else instead.

Problems with distractibility tend to affect sleep hygiene as well, which bleeds into job performance and other life-coping mechanisms. Research suggests that 80 percent of adults with ADD/ADHD suffer from some form of poor sleep hygiene. This may include difficulty going to sleep, staying asleep, getting restful sleep or being able to get up in the morning.

Combining sleep issues with ADD/ADHD creates a perfect storm of distractibility at the office. The result often leads to missed deadlines, unfinished tasks and gaining a reputation for unreliability. This workplace stress creates an additional burden for the wives of these men, who live with the constant fear that their husbands will lose their job. Medication offers a partial solution, at best. Many wives report that while medication may help their husbands function better at work, it wears off soon after they come home.

Tracey C., a children's agent in Hollywood, described her husband's nighttime routine, as she watches him revert to his "normal" ADD self.

When he gets home from work during the week, all I want him to do is to take 30 minutes or so with the kids while I make dinner. But he's always got a list of two hundred projects he's started that he thinks he needs to get done right then. He rarely spends more than 10 or 20 minutes with our kids during the week.

Given the all-encompassing nature of the challenge, wives who want to help their husbands gain a handle on their distracted nature face an uphill battle. However, as therapists gain more understanding of ADD/ADHD and how to work with it, three distinct strategies appear to produce positive results.

First, adopting certain behaviors will help ADD/ADHD men function more efficiently. Second, both partners can agree to alter their attitudes with regard to ADD/ADHD and its implications. Third, life choices should be crafted in ways that work with the husband's situation, rather than trying to change his core being. The wife of a man with ADD/ADHD should understand that his condition is here to stay. However, learning to channel it productively can mean the difference between a marriage beset by problems and frustration and one that thrives on the acceptance of each other's limitations—and unique talents.

With regard to helpful behaviors, researchers and coaches suggest a number of simple coping strategies. For example, when conversing with others, men with ADD/ADHD should remain aware of their tendency to blurt out unrelated comments, and that they often express their wandering thoughts out loud.

One way to deal with this is simply to let the other person know that there is another participant in the conversation, namely the ADD/ADHD. This allows both parties to adjust to this reality. Even taking the time to jot down the topics to be covered will help both parties redirect their focus and stay on the subject at hand. Maintaining eye contact or even a quick touch also helps improve focus.

At work, men with ADD/ADHD should institute certain practices to reduce the level of the distractions that interfere with their workflow during the day. Some suggestions:

- Transfer phone calls to voice mail automatically
- Block email access until set hours of the day
- Arrange the work day into efficient blocks of time that allow projects to be completed, or divided into discrete units of focus.

Beyond the behavioral strategies, husbands and wives should take time to think about ADD from the 30,000-foot level, as opposed to constantly occupying their thoughts with the details. In other words, viewing the distractibility associated with ADD/ADHD in a new light may play a significant role in reducing the amount of stress and tension caused by the condition.

Timothy D. Wilson is a Professor of Psychology at the University of Virginia and the author of *Redirect: The Surprising New Science of Psychological Change*. In this book, he argues that people have the power to change their lives by creating new narratives about their experiences and behavior. Professor Wilson refers to this practice as "story editing," and it holds out a lot of hope for couples whose relationships are affected by ADD/ADHD. He recommends, for example, that wives "edit out" the assumption that their husbands don't care for them by creating a new, equally truthful, narrative about their relationship. Focusing on the idea that ADD/ADHD originates in neurobiological differences in the brain can help diffuse many of the strong emotions associated with certain behaviors. It helps to create an atmosphere of acceptance and solution-seeking, rather than blaming and finger-pointing.

A word of caution: crafting a new narrative takes time and guidance. It must ring true to all parties. As such, it pays to approach a counselor who focuses on narrative therapy in order to gain the most out of this strategy.

Finally, both wives and husbands should understand that life with ADD/ADHD represents the ultimate flex-time experience. Men with ADD will most likely never fit into the traditional 9–5 role. The good news is that the world of work appears to be shifting away from that model in favor of a much more flexible arrangement. Furthermore, men with ADD/ADHD offer a number of positive qualities, often overlooked, but nevertheless useful and necessary to many aspects of career success. One of those positive qualities is creativity. Others include the desire for action, change, speed, and fun. Properly channeled, these qualities can result in any number of positive outlets, such as art, music, computers, and even extreme sports.

In the end, wives who help their husbands discover and tap into and channel their inner passion will often find that the distractibility diminishes once these men have found their true path. In its place, they just may find themselves married to the happy, passionate, and successful man of their dreams.

Disorganization

As the old saying goes, "The best way to get nothing done is to try to do everything at once." For non-ADD/ADHD adults, the phrase strikes a familiar, humorous chord that reminds us to rein things in when we find ourselves running off in all directions at once.

For men with ADD/ADHD, this phrase encapsulates how they live their lives. When these men are single, the quirks associated with being chronically disorganized may not impact the people around them. After all, no one has to see their bedroom, their kitchen or even their car. Once they get married, though, the disorganization that comes with ADD/ADHD certainly affects people negatively—most notably, their wives!

To be sure, successful marriages thrive on romance, love, and a nurturing environment. At the same time, most marriages operate as intricate psychological, emotional and logistical systems that require both parties to pull their own weight. Dishes need to be washed, laundry needs to be done, bills need to be paid. Mail and magazines need to be sorted. The list goes on and on. To most people, the daily upkeep of a home comes with the territory. But to the wives of men with ADD/ADHD, getting their husbands to take care of even the simplest of tasks presents a nearly insurmountable challenge.

The result? You guessed it: Anger, frustration and, eventually, hopelessness as the understanding sinks in that their husbands may never change. These words ring particularly true with Melinda D., a photographer, who lives just outside of Austin, Texas.

At this point, I don't want amazing. All I want is someone to do the dishes once in a while!

She went on to explain that certain tasks, such as cleaning the kitchen, paying the bills, or picking up the kids for school are "not optional" for her—but they are for her husband. In his disorganized approach to life, spending hours in the garage working on a project takes on equal importance with doing what needs to be done around the house. To make matters worse, even when her husband attempts to help out, his chronic disorganization usually does more harm than good.

One time he threw some clothes in the wash to help me out. He promptly forgot all about them and left them there wet so long that they wound up mildewing the washer. A utility bill that he 'assured' me had been paid had, of course, not been paid. We almost had our power shut off because of him.

The disorganization associated with ADD/ADHD seeps into nearly every area of life. Wives whose husbands have ADD/ADHD find themselves watching with disbelief as the men they loves constantly misplace routine items, purchase things more than once after misplacing the first one or find their workspaces buried under a mountain of junk. Phone messages go ignored, paperwork gets lost, and keys go missing for days. Furthermore, most attempts at solving the predicament fall on deaf ears. Joanna H. from Indianapolis, Indiana, describes her husband this way:

I've been married seven long years. I work full time. I have a three-year-old to take care of—and a 40-year-old teenager.

At one point, in utter frustration, she created a chart system that listed both her and her husband's household chores.

I learned that if you put down, 'do the dishes,' that does not necessarily translate into cleaning the countertops, table, and putting the kitchen back in order. He thought putting dishes in the dishwasher and turning it on was enough—no matter what the kitchen actually looked like at the end. Needless to say, the charts did not last too long.

Given this daily frustration, many partners face an overwhelming temptation just to give up. Nevertheless, the situation is not completely without hope. Yes, expecting perfection is unrealistic. But this does not preclude making small improvements to create a more manageable situation. In fact, moving from chaos to ordinary messiness should be regarded as a major victory in the "war on disorganization."

As a first step, wives should remember that the disorganization associated with ADD/ADHD starts in their husbands' minds. After all, there's a whirlwind swirling around up there. That's why taking the whirlwind out of his head and putting it onto a piece of paper is a key, first strategy in gaining control over chaos. To accomplish this, plan things out on paper, preferably in short to-do lists. Stay away from fancy computer software programs. Nothing creates more opportunities for interruptions than placing an ADD/ADHD husband in front of a computer. As the saying goes, "If it's worth remembering, it's worth writing down."

Second, most experts recommend limiting the to-do list to the top three priorities. Focusing on three major tasks each day helps keep the flow of the household moving in an organized fashion. Once the tasks have been completed, that's it for the day. Do not allow your husband to shift into "hyperfocus" mode in which he begins to move obsessively through an endless list of tasks. Sooner, rather than later, he will tire of this shiny new project, leaving a trail of half-finished tasks in its wake. Include an estimate of how long each item on the to-do list should take. A word to the wise: apply the Rule of 1.5 to any time estimates. Assume any task will take that much longer than originally planned.

Third, with regard to clutter, start by making sure every object has a "home," a place where it goes, now and forever. Once again, instituting a "home-base" system forces the disorganized ADD/ADHD husband to create order outside of his brain. Keys go on the key hook, wallets on the dresser, coats in the closet. It may be helpful for a wife to post reminders along her husband's "entry path" as he comes through the door.

More than a key swing state in Presidential elections, OHIO offers yet another strategy to help reduce clutter. OHIO stands for "Only Handle It Once," and it is a great tool for getting rid of junk mail. It also reduces the likelihood that bills will get paid on time. To be sure, many wives may not want their ADD/ADHD husbands to handle the mail at all. Nevertheless, he can still apply the OHIO rule by agreeing either to let his wife bring the mail in (as tempting as it may be to look at each and every "interesting" item when he finds it in the mailbox), or to handle the mail once—by giving it to his wife.

A fourth aspect related to clearing clutter has to do with ridding the house of unwanted papers, magazines, tools—and just assorted stuff that accumulates over time. One wife explained that when it comes to reducing clutter in the house, she simply decided to take matters into her own hands. "My husband used to get mad at me if I threw things away or put everything into one pile," said Terri S., an ice-skating instructor in Minneapolis, Minnesota. Now she gives her husband two days to go through all of his paper junk. After two days, Terri places everything in a plastic box and leaves it in the garage. When the box is full she throws the contents away. The plan leaves everyone happier. "By that time he's forgotten about it, anyway," she said.

Remember, ADD/ADHD men resist schedules and routines. Even a wife's best-laid plans may go astray if the to-do lists turn into a jail cell of obligations. Though many wives may believe that nagging only counts when it is said out loud, their ADD/ADHD husbands might argue that a post-it note can contain plenty of nagging of its own.

Dr. Jaksa, the clinical psychologist from Chicago, recommends a multi-layered approach to helping husbands maintain their enthusiasm about becoming more organized over the long haul.

First, make the process as entertaining as possible. Dishes, for example, can get just as clean—maybe even cleaner—with good music playing in the background. Rewarding small victories also increases motivation. Second, help your husband visualize the benefits of conquering disorganization. It may even be useful to create an actual dream board around this goal. Finally, men with ADD/ADHD need to understand that living an organized life is much more than adopting a restrictive set of rules. Instead, living an organized life allows a person to pursue all sorts of activities and dreams he never had time for before. Indeed, for the ADD/ADHD man, organization is liberation.

Information Overload

Many men with ADD/ADHD have difficulty managing the flow of information within their brain. One reason for this ongoing challenge is that they often take on too many tasks at once. Their brains run on constant overdrive, processing information much faster than others. As a result, they seek to fill the space in their brain in order to keep it occupied.

The problem is that the brain dislikes absorbing information too rapidly for too long. This leads to a keen battle between the different aspects of the ADD/ADHD brain. One part of the brain craves new information. Another worries about overload. An apt metaphor for this process is the relationship between hunger and food. Like the brain, the stomach can only take in so much food before it starts to become full, causing discomfort. Most people sense when they have eaten too much and know how to stop – at least in theory. In fact, people who lack the ability to feel full suffer from constant hunger, even though their stomach cannot take any more food.

The same idea applies to men with ADD/ADHD. They lack the ability to discern when their brains are full. Without developing this skill of recognition, they will continue to feel exhausted, tired, fatigued, and unsatisfied because they are unconsciously allowing their brains to operate in a state of constant burden. A man with ADD/ADHD may spend hours on the Internet, opening up one new page after another, until he reaches the point where he has more than 20 tabs open at once. This is clearly "over-eating" for the brain. In the end, he winds up closing his browser altogether because he cannot handle processing all that information at one time. Similarly, men with ADD/ADHD often abandon projects in midstream because they have substituted filling their brain with information for actually getting something done.

A useful tactic in dealing with this tendency is to recognize how the brain feels when it is approaching information overload and to take steps to slow down the process. For example, opening five tabs open on a browser provides more than enough information for any one person to absorb at any one time. Beyond that, the brain starts to go into overload. A person can train himself to become aware when he is putting too much into his brain, how much the brain can absorb, and at what point he feels full. Mastering this technique takes time, and will not happen overnight. Working with a professional ADD/ADHD therapist or coach can be a great help to those who have this problem.

[5]

Intention Deficit Disorder

Though it may not be politically correct to say so in this day and age, the truth is that one word separates the men from the boys: motivation. This is true when men compare themselves to other men, and it is true when they compare themselves to their personal ideal of what they could and should be "when they grow up."

Whether they say so or not, their wives understand this, too. Most women look up to a man who has ambition as well as the motivation to follow through on his goals. Men with ADD/ADHD often score well in the ambition department. Many goals emerge from their particular way of being in the world. Follow-through, however, is another story.

Richard C. is a case in point. As a writer who took eight years to complete his first novel, Richard acknowledges he has a distinct challenge when it comes to maintaining the motivation to finish what he starts.

I once told my brothers, 'I don't do endings.' I have a passion for writing and have written quite a lot, but most of it is unfinished. Sometimes it's the sheer number of ideas I have that keeps me from following through on any single one. With writing, I have two files full of ideas, and they are each over one hundred pages long.

His challenge with motivation extends to mundane tasks as well.

Piles sit for months and even years before I somehow get to cleaning them. Motivation seems impossible. It's like the planets have to be in alignment, or something.

Many wives of men with ADD/ADHD will recognize more than a bit of their husband in Richard's words. However, the lack of motivation exhibited by men with ADD/ADHD differs from that of the garden-variety slacker. It is one thing not to want to set the world on fire. Making a lifetime career out of it is something else altogether.

Carol D. works as an office manager at a busy medical clinic just outside Syracuse, New York. Watching her husband's continued lack of motivation has brought her to the breaking point of considering divorce.

He acts like teenager. All he wants to do is play video games and talk about electronics. There is no sense of actually doing something productive with his life. I'm starting to hate my life with him.

As often happens when women lose respect for their husbands, Carol's disdain is spilling over into the bedroom. She admits she no longer finds her husband attractive and increasingly avoids being intimate with him.

Other women complain that even when their husbands find jobs, they lose them quickly.

I've been married to my husband for more than 12 years. In that time he has had no less than a dozen jobs—each ending pretty quickly—with him quitting after getting angry at some issue or another. I'm left holding the bag trying to pay the bills and take care of all of his projects and hobbies that keep coming and going.

-- Marcia S., New York City

Though it may come as little consolation, most men with ADD/ADHD are not oblivious to their actions in this arena. In fact, they walk through life acutely aware of their struggle. Furthermore, even if their wives refrain from criticizing them, they still find themselves haunted by the voices of teachers, parents, and other significant people from their past. Words like "lazy," "unmotivated," and "worthless" make up a large portion of the "tapes" they carry around in their heads. And, to be honest, they have a hard time disproving these characterizations.

Charles T., who lives outside Akron, Ohio, echoed Marcia's sentiments.

I can't tell you how many jobs I've quit just because I can't be bothered. For whatever reason, I can't seem to stick to any job. There are times when I've quit in a matter of days, others in weeks or months.

Other men with ADD/ADHD voiced their own frustration over their inability to focus on meaningful tasks. In some cases, coasting through long stretches of simply doing nothing almost becomes a way of life. "I literally do not get anything done for weeks, even months," said Tom M., who has a degree in computer animation. "I just surf the net, play games, and do random things all day."

When it comes to men with ADD/ADHD, the question is why this particular disorder strikes so deeply at their ability to muster up sufficient motivation to function normally in society. Is it simply a matter of laziness or immaturity? If men like Charles and Tom recognize that their days are spent in useless activity, why can't they change?

The answer starts with an understanding of how human motivation actually works. Zig Ziglar, a popular sales and motivational trainer himself, once described motivation as "the fuel necessary to keep the human engine running."

Some may dismiss Mr. Ziglar's words as little more than a catchphrase best suited for a bumper sticker. However, it turns out that his insight touches on certain physiological realities—as opposed to psycho-

logical realities—that appear to have been confirmed by leading researchers in the field of ADD/ADHD.

A study published by the *Journal of the American Medical Association (JAMA)* appeared to support a neurogenic link between ADD/ADHD and a lack of motivation. The study, conducted at Brookhaven National Laboratory and headed by researcher Nora Volkow, MD, found that individuals with ADD/ADHD lack a key protein in the brain, which plays a role in the human capacity to experience reward and motivation. Adults with ADD/ADHD suffer from a deficit in the way they process dopamine, a neurotransmitter that assists humans in anticipating pleasure and reward, which is a key component in creating motivation to achieve a goal.

It is always controversial to link what appears to be a character flaw to a chemical imbalance. Nevertheless, the study's findings do offer insight into many of the difficulties experienced by men with ADD/ADHD—and, of course, the accompanying frustration felt by their wives. If a dopamine deficit reduces human motivation, it is a bit easier to understand why men with ADD/ADHD become so easily bored or distracted, why they have a history of being hard to teach in school, and why they tend to jump from job to job. Put simply, these tasks offer no immediate gratification, so there is no reason for the man with ADD/ADHD to bother.

Research by Dr. Russell Barkley adds some dimensions to these findings. According to Dr. Barkley, men with ADD/ADHD are not stupid. They know what they need to do to complete a given task or achieve a certain goal. However, they lack the executive functioning skills necessary to put what they know into action.

Speaking at The Centre for ADHD/ADD Advocacy Canada (CADDAC) before a group of experts on the topic, Dr. Barkley described the challenge faced by individuals with ADD/ADHD. "The problem is at the point of performance in implementing what they know," he said. He went on to pinpoint the source of the problem as originating in the brain's motor function, rather than sensory function.

When a distracting event provokes a response in a non-ADD/ADHD individual, the brain knows how to suppress and filter out these irrelevant events. People with ADD/ADHD, by contrast, respond to such distraction by "running off on a chain of tangential thinking." Not only that, but they fail to return to the task at hand. The distracting event "destroys the capacity to hold information in the mind," Dr. Barkley explained.

Those who do not have ADD/ADHD think about goals and motivation. They know how to aim their behavior ahead in time and how to employ skills such as persistence and motivation, because they sense the reward at the end of the tunnel, so to speak. Men with ADD/ADHD lack this ability. They literally do not feel it.

Given their inability to conjure up internal motivation, men with ADD/ADHD will always be dependent on external consequences to achieve long-term goals. This is why—even as adults—they can play video games for hours. Video games provide external, continuous reinforcement. The consequences are tied directly to the actions and delivered in real time. Doing homework or executing a longer-term task at work, on the other hand, has no immediate consequences, and therefore, no motivational meaning for a man with ADD/ADHD. This has several implications in terms of how wives of men with ADD/ADHD can help their husbands overcome this challenge.

As Dr. Barkley explained, reward needs to be tied as closely as possible to the performance of the task. This means that talking about goals and improvement literally falls on deaf ears. Instead, men with ADD/ADHD need to create a system that grants them continuous reward on the way to achieving the overall goal. Imagine a bird walking through a path of breadcrumbs in the forest, eating the crumbs as she moves toward her goal. The same holds true, in concept, for instilling motivation in men with ADD/ADHD. In practical terms, this could mean breaking a task into separate, easy-to-achieve goals.

One therapist suggests finding ways to inject interest challenge, urgency, or novelty into the task. As an example, suppose the husband is responsible for paying the household bills, but he finds it too boring to complete, especially if it takes place in a secluded office. Instead, she recommends doing the bills in a coffee shop, where the surroundings will, ironically, offer just enough "distraction" to allow the husband to complete the task in one sitting.

Wives should not expect their husbands to suddenly develop an internal motivational drive. Expecting this to happen is a recipe for years of frustration. Instead, much more mileage can be gained by creating external motivators that help husbands stay on task.

[6]

Time Myopia

sk anyone who has attended a local meeting of CHADD (Children and Adults with Attention Deficit Disorders), and they will most likely tell you just how often the topic of "handling time" comes up for couples dealing with ADD/ADHD.

A moment's reflection will demonstrate why this is so: Time is the only thing we all share. We exist in time. We run our lives according to its rules. From waking up in the morning, to getting on a plane, to finishing an assignment, to knowing when to stop one thing and move on to the next, the ability to use time effectively is one of the hallmarks of successful living. When you throw our over-stimulated, multi-tasking society into the mix, it becomes clear that time is the most precious commodity we have. In fact, survey after survey shows that people consider a lack of time—even more than a lack of money—one of the most vexing problems of our generation.

Men with ADD/ADHD rarely grasp this stark fact of life. Instead, they walk through the world basically blind—or at least myopic—to time, and it can drive their wives crazy.

Larissa W., a kindergarten teacher in Oconomowoc, Wisconsin, described how it feels trying to deal with her husband's time myopia on a daily basis.

The only way I can describe it is tunnel vision. Sometimes he can't get anything done. But when he is in his 'productive mode' he focuses like a maniac—but only on one thought or one action.

As an example, she explained what it is like to watch her husband clean the bathroom.

The rest of the house could be on fire, but that bathroom is going to get cleaned. It could take hours, and there's no talking him out of it.

To add to Larissa's aggravation, her husband "can't" talk to her while he is involved in one of his "focus-manias" until he has finished.

Not that it serves as any consolation, but men with ADD/ADHD frequently acknowledge that the "all or nothing" relationship to time described by Larissa fits them to a T.

Richard C, a salesman in Orange County, California, described the moments when he "appears to be doing nothing," as simply being "overwhelmed."

If I look like I'm doing nothing, I'm probably going over the monstrous to-do list swimming around in my brain. When that happens, I don't know where to begin. I turn around and think, 'What did I just accomplish with the last four hours of my life? Wait—that was four hours???'

As with many of the symptoms associated with ADD/ADHD, time myopia is not necessarily a reflection of poor character or a lack of discipline. When it comes to time management skills, each person possesses an internal clock measuring how much time has passed on a given task. Some people judge the passage of time with uncanny accuracy. Others, less so, but a common thread among functional people is the ability to gauge time, create new priorities to fit available time, and recalibrate their schedules to fit the needs of the day.

According to Dr. Barkley, for men with ADD/ADHD their internal clock remains stuck on snooze. As a result, they lack the means to shift focus when necessary. Their lives lurch from one crisis to the next. Dr. Barkley's advice to men with ADD/ADHD, and their wives, is to recognize that the solution begins with understanding the nature of the problem. Since, as we have mentioned, the problem derives from a lack of executive functioning, the solution should incorporate the artificial creation of executive functioning skills when they are most needed.

With regard to time myopia, the problem is an over-cluttered mind combined with a faulty time-tracking mechanism. Therefore, the first step in overcoming this challenge is to clear as much information out of the mind as possible. This means helping your husband put key pieces of information into some kind of physical form and making sure he has access to it when needed.

For example, if your husband's boss has given him a project to complete within a certain number of days, forget about verbally encouraging him to remember the deadline. Instead, have him keep a running to-do list, with the steps needed to finish discrete tasks on the way to completing the overall project. Researchers refer to this process as creating an "external working memory."

Another helpful strategy is to take the concept of time—which, after all, has no physical reality—and make it as physically tangible as possible. Clocks, timers, reminder-texts, and the like can be set to break down blocks of time into useful units.

The same holds true for the smaller tasks that make up a person's daily routine. For example, Post-It notes in the kitchen can let your husband know that breakfast finishes by 8:30 a.m. Certain household items can be set on timers, such as lights, the computer, the Internet browser, etc. By creating a system that automatically turns things off, you will help your husband break his hyperfocus episodes and enable him to move on to other important tasks.

It is also helpful to realize that successful time management requires sufficient time to transition from one task to another. ADD/ADHD men are notorious for believing they can do everything all at once. For example, they tend to be constantly surprised at the realization that getting from one place to another actually requires time.

Ari Tuckman, a counselor who works with ADD/ADHD clients and the author of *The ADHD Executive Functions Workbook*, encourages his clients to add at least 50 percent more time to all estimates of how long a certain task should take. Though this hint may sound simple in concept, weaving it into practice requires discipline. The payoff in terms of increased calmness is well worth the effort.

Since ADD/ADHD men tend to suffer from a hurried mind, one of the most important goals of time management is learning how to help the mind slow down. While the previous strategies we described will be helpful on a behavioral level, "Mindfulness" addresses the issue on a deeper level.

There are differing opinions as to whether it is possible to achieve Mindfulness in the absence of medication. Many believe that correcting the neurological deficits associated with ADD/ADHD requires medication. Others, like Yongey Mingyur Rinpoche, the author of *The Joy of Living: Unlocking the Secret and Science of Happiness*, believe that this practice can be made accessible to all, without medication.

In its most basic form, Mindfulness calls for a person to notice the workings of the mind in the present moment. If the mind wanders, the individual is trained to gently bring it back to the moment. The benefit for men with ADD/ADHD is that they are permitted to continue to daydream and shift focus. However, when that happens, they are encouraged to notice it and remind themselves of the task at hand.

Lidia Zylowska, M.D. is the author of *The Mindfulness Prescription for Adult ADHD* as well as numerous other books and studies on the topic. One of the tools she uses to help adults with ADD/ADHD gain greater control over their thought process is derived from the acronym STOP, which she outlined in an interview with Stephanie Sarkis Ph.D., in *Psychology Today.*

In this strategy, each letter acts as a reminder to simultaneously slow down, while moving forward to control the distraction. S stands for Stop, (i.e., to pause for a moment before acting). T stands for Take a deep breath, which helps slow both the mind and body. O calls for the individual to observe himself in the moment, particularly with regard to body sensations and current action. P means to proceed – but with more relaxation and the awareness that actions may in fact be done as a matter of choice, rather than compulsion.

To be sure, this can take practice. However, implementing some aspects of Mindfulness into a routine can help men with ADD/ADHD set a pattern of slowing down the pace of their thoughts. This, in turn, helps develop clearer thinking patterns, which can pave the way for more harmonious interactions in handling the many "little" tasks that are a part of everyday life – and every marriage.

PART 2

THE IMPACT

OF ADD/ADHD

[7]

Emotions

Shame is one of the core human emotions. However, not all shame is created equal. There are three types of shame: healthy shame, guilt, and Toxic Shame. Though they are often used interchangeably, shame, and guilt are two very different concepts. People generally experience guilt when they have made a mistake accepted by society as wrong. An example would be breaking the law, coming to work late, or cheating on your spouse. With regard to this type of error, taking corrective action (e.g., admitting the wrong-doing) also helps assuage a person's feelings of guilt.

Healthy shame occurs when we find ourselves in an embarrassing situation. Forgetting to zip up your fly after using the bathroom causes healthy shame. Healthy shame or embarrassment usually dissipates quickly. Toxic Shame, on the other hand, is more intense and prolonged, and it is almost always associated with feelings of worthlessness. It penetrates to the very core of a person and encompasses much more than simple mistakes.

By way of illustration, it is normal to feel guilty about being late for work. If this becomes a habit, however, the guilt may transform into shame over a lack of discipline, laziness and maturity. If this goes on for years—or even decades—without any improvement (as is the case with many men with ADD/ADHD), the individual is likely to feel a deep sense of shame over what he perceives to be a basic inadequacy, low self-esteem and worthlessness.

Imagine what it was like for your husband to grow up in a world where nearly every adult pointed a finger at him as the "bad child," the one who constantly misbehaved, caused trouble, never listened, never finished what he started and never overcame his laziness. Those messages do not easily disappear. They get woven into the fabric of a person's psyche and become the soundtrack to his life.

For years, Tim K., a loan officer in Burlington, Vermont, tried to deny his ADD/ADHD. However, even after he acknowledged his condition, he continued to face difficult challenges.

The hardest thing I've had to deal with was getting my spouse and other family [members] to understand that a mental or emotional disorder, such as ADD/ADHD, depression or anxiety, can be just as debilitating as any physical disability—if not worse. I mean, if you have a heart attack or just break a bone, it's obvious to those around you that you have a genuine medical problem. But with ADD/ADHD, there is no cast, or x-rays. On the outside everything looks normal. It's easier to dismiss your problems as laziness, contrariness, or whatever excuse is handy, rather than to take the time to figure out what's really going on. Imagine telling a stroke victim to 'just deal with it,' or 'if you really cared, you'd get it done.'

Children with ADD/ADHD (and remember that if your husband has ADD/ADHD an as adult, he had it as a child, too), often express the feeling that their parents don't really love them. This rarely stems from neglect. Rather, this is the byproduct of being on the receiving end of being told how "bad" or "wrong" or "lazy" they are. Eventually, these children—and they adults that they grow into—question whether it is possible for any parent to love a child with these deficiencies. Often, this sense of shame expresses itself as anger towards others.

David C., an unemployed trucker living outside of Des Moines, Iowa, went more than 36 years before being diagnosed with ADD/ADHD.

I wish the answers available to me now, were available to me then. My life would have been drastically different.

He still carries a lot of resentment over his past.

I was labeled your typical problem child. I cried many nights not knowing why I was acting the way I was, but [I] also realized it didn't stop but only got worse over time.

As an adult, David admits having difficulty breaking the coping habits he learned as a child.

For years I lashed out at anyone who dared get in my face—and whew, temper, temper! I still feel the need to protect myself this way, and I can't stand it.

If your husband was one of the lucky ones whose parents were pro-active about getting him tested early on, and perhaps even had him put on medication, then he may not feel the same intense shame felt by his peers with ADD/ADHD. However, even if he grew up in the most supportive environment possible, your husband, having grown up with ADD/ADHD, will still spend his life questioning if he will ever become the man he hopes to be: one who can focus on completing tasks, who is emotionally available to his partner, and who can bring organization into his mind and into his life.

Depression

Depression is a common medical disorder that affects feelings, thoughts, and actions. Symptoms of depression range from changes in appetite to attempted suicide. Depression is NOT situational, meaning it is not the low feeling a person has after a bad day at work. Depression is much more complex and debilitating. People with depression must show signs from the following list of symptoms for longer than two weeks before being considered for a diagnosis by a doctor:

- Deep feeling of sadness
- Less interest or pleasure in usual activities or hobbies
- Insomnia or oversleeping
- Feelings of worthlessness or inappropriate guilt
- Trouble making decisions or concentrating
- Low energy or feeling tired, even when you are not active
- Changes in appetite which cause weight loss/gain
- Thoughts of death or suicide or attempts at suicide

Much like ADD/ADHD, depression reflects a chemical imbalance in the brain, rather than a defect in personality or character. A normally functioning brain works like a computer, which sends messages to all the different parts of the body and controls everything from heartbeat to walking to emotions. Billions of nerve cells in the brain, known as neurons, act as conductors for the brain's messages. Neurons send and receive messages from the rest of the body via specific chemicals known as neurotransmitters. Depression occurs when these neurotransmitters fail to correctly send and receive messages between brain cells. Depression is a common "co-morbid" disorder for people with ADD/ADHD, which means that people ADD/ADHD often suffer from depression at the same time.

Anxiety

Anxiety is also an issue for people with ADD/ADHD. Without therapy, people with ADD/ADHD rarely keep calendars, wear a watch, or have an organized system for keeping appointments, to-do's, etc. Imagine trying to keep all the information stored in your head. That's what the mind of someone with ADD/ADHD is constantly trying to manage, and it is a losing battle. For many men with ADD/ADHD, this results in a life of constant stress and anxiety. High stress leads to fatigue, which leads to forgetfulness, which only complicates the problem.

Anxiety is also an issue because people with ADD/ADHD often fear that they will never be able to get their life on track. Feeling stressed out all the time over their inability to complete simple tasks, when everyone else around them seems able to do so with ease, further increases the anxiety felt by people with ADD/ADHD. In extreme cases, this anxiety can build up over time and bubble over into Anxiety (or Panic Attacks). At the Sachs Center we recommend Cognitive Behavioral Therapy to reduce the symptoms of anxiety (which we will talk about more in Chapter 15).

Addiction

People with ADD/ADHD often suffer from poor academic marks as children and low professional performance as adults. As mentioned previously, this often leads to low self-esteem, which has been linked with substance abuse. There are several reasons for this, including apathy about self-care, wanting to feel good, disregard for personal health, etc. Additionally, it can also be more difficult for people with ADD/ADHD to form and keep meaningful relationships, which leads to loneliness, isolation and withdrawal.

Even in a married or committed relationship, men with ADD/ADHD experience these emotions and turn to substance abuse as a coping mechanism. Physiologically, people with ADD/ADHD may suffer from an ineffective transmission of dopamine in sensitive areas of the brain. The lower level of dopamine produced by men with ADD/ADHD may lead them to try to compensate or "self-medicate" for this deficiency through substance abuse. In other words, because men with ADD/ADHD experience difficulty in feeling the normal pleasures of life, they may seek out alcohol, drugs, thrill-seeking experiences, or excessive amounts of food to compensate for this lack.

Even if they avoid substance abuse, many men with ADD/ADHD become addicted to certain junk foods. Sugar, for example, represents one of the major categories of food addictions found among these men. This, too, traces its roots to a chemical deficiency. Research shows that the ADD/ADHD brain absorbs glucose more slowly than normal. As a result, many men with ADD/ADHD binge on foods with high sugar and carbohydrate levels. All of these are quick fixes for a larger problem, and none of them will actually improve the ADD/ADHD-sufferer's quality of life in the long run.

Treatment for addiction with someone who has ADD/ADHD looks a bit different than traditional substance abuse treatment. For any addiction treatment to work, treatment must integrate therapies for addiction management and symptoms management. Treating either condition in isolation will not work. Treating only the addiction without treating ADD/ADHD in conjunction with it will quickly lead to relapse and abuse. Untreated addiction alone will significantly worsen ADD/ADHD symptoms. If your husband is addicted, talk to him (or his therapist) to make sure he is telling the whole story about his addiction. He can only get the help he needs if the therapist knows the whole truth about your husband's physical and mental health practices.

[8]

Relationships

Functioning at work demands organization as well as well-maintained behavior, time management, self-organization, problem-solving abilities, and self-motivation. If your husband is one of those men who cannot seem to focus and follow through on a business idea, or who is constantly being reprimanded at the workplace, or even given the boot, his ADD/ADHD may be the reason.

A study published in The Archives of Clinical Neuropsychology in 2010 sought to determine whether ADD/ADHD can be linked to deficits in executive functioning (EF) by looking at the degree of impairment in 11 measures involving self-reported occupational problems, employer-reported workplace adjustment, and clinician-rated occupational adjustment.

The research team, from the University of South Carolina, divided subjects into three groups: those with diagnosed ADD/ADHD, those with some symptoms but no diagnosis, and a control group. When compared with the latter two groups, adults with diagnosed ADD/ADHD were found to have (a) had more trouble with other employees, (b) behavior problems, (c) been fired, (d) quit out of boredom, and (e) been disciplined by a supervisor. Employers rated the ADD/ADHD group as having greater problems with inattentiveness compared to the other two groups, despite having had no knowledge of the diagnoses.

The conclusion reached from the research was that people with ADD/ADHD exhibit poorer overall performance at work, which could lead to a range of social, personal, and financial problems in the long run.

Working with an ADD/ADHD Coach for men with significant problems in the workplace can be very helpful. Executives of major companies, who don't struggle with ADD/ADHD, pay consultants to assist them in learning time management and organizational techniques. If they can improve their skills, so can your husband. Google "ADD Coach" or "Executive Coach" to find someone in your area.

In The Bedroom

He swept you off your feet. Part Prince Charming, part superhero, the man you fell in love with seemed like a dream come true at first. His intense interest in you and the hyperfocus on your relationship filled your love life with playfulness, fulfillment, and joy.

That was then. This is now.

For many women married to men with ADD/ADHD, intimacy is one of the most challenging aspects of the relationship. A couple's sex life can often be a barometer of the relationship in general. Every couple experiences ups and downs, but a healthy marriage has the potential to create peace in the home that allows each partner to smooth over the rough patches. The opposite is also true. A rancorous relationship outside the bedroom will adversely affect a couple's ability to relate to each other sexually. For various reasons, women tend to be more sensitive to the relationship barometer and its effect on intimacy than their husbands.

Adding into the mix a partner with ADD/ADHD makes life even more complicated. In many instances, the husband's inability to create a warm, affectionate and loving sex life with his wife can be the straw that breaks the camel's back. It is almost as if all the negative effects of ADD/ADHD play themselves out in a concentrated form, leaving the wife struggling to find any escape she can from her already overloaded and overwhelmed daily life. The following account describes one wife's view of the way in which her and her ADD/ADHD husband's sex life deteriorated over the years:

> When my husband and were first going out, he was like a dog with a bone, no pun intended. We had sex constantly. It was fun, because we were still new to each other and were still exploring each other's bodies. But after the first six months, the curiosity and excitement died away on his part. I felt as though he wasn't interested in my body anymore. I would go out of my way to pleasure him, but he would hardly ever go out of his way for me. In time, sex became rote. There was virtually no foreplay. I was a piece of meat, not something to be romanced. Sex for him can last about five minutes to be effective, but if it lasts more than ten to fifteen minutes he gives up because chances are he's not going to climax and whether I could or not isn't even in question. When he touches me, he is lackluster and lazy, to the point where I almost want to yell at him, 'You're not even TRYING!'

Cheryl tried talking to her husband about their situation, but she held back from fully communicating out of fear that it would destroy his sense of virility—and ultimately their marriage.

My husband and I do love each other very much, and are still very much attracted to each other, but those things don't always account for sexual chemistry, which is very hard to cultivate when one body is trying to communicate with another, but the other isn't listening,

Cheryl's experience is not unique. Often the wife of a man affected by ADD/ADHD is surprised to find out that the man she married— the same guy who could not get enough of her during their courtship— loses significant interest in her shortly after the wedding. In many cases, his loss of sexual interest happens naturally as a result of his condition, because once something becomes normalized in his life, he impulsively exchanges it for something more "shiny."

When this is applied to his attitude toward their sex life, the shiny replacement for intimacy and love-making with his wife is often the quick high of masturbating to online pornography. Considering that eight out of ten men admit to watching porn within the past year, this is more likely the case for the man with ADD/ADHD, because pornography can easily be found on the Internet (often for free) and offers an unending supply of "shiny" sexual toys. This only compounds the wife's sense of betrayal, loneliness and frustration when she finds out that her husband has plenty of interest in sex—just not in real sex, and not with her.

Janet M., a personal trainer in Galveston, Texas, had no qualms about stating exactly how she felt.

For my part, dear (ex-) hubby treated me like a blow-up doll. I was there solely for his own instant sexual gratification. It was like he had a whole misfire in his brain on the idea that intimacy is different from sex, which made our love life completely unenjoyable for me. It was as if I had to explain to him that I'm not one of the nameless

girls from the porn sites you obsess about, and that I did not want to
be treated the same way an alcoholic treats a bottle of booze."

In other instances, the couple's sexual problems have nothing to do with an addiction to pornography. Instead, life in the bedroom is simply an extension of the husband's everyday ADD symptoms.

There are times when we will be right in the middle of getting hot
and heavy, and he will just stop and start talking about some ran-
dom, trivial thing that has nothing to do with anything, and I have to
start all over again.

--- Kirsten H., Orange Country, California.

A similar complaint was voiced by Wendy H., a photographer in up-state New York. She readily admits that her husband means well, but his ADD/ADHD symptoms take control of his good intentions.

My husband is very self-aware. A few times he's lost his erection and
has told me that it's not me; it's that he starts stressing about per-
forming, pleasing me, etc., and then it snowballs until his mind is so
busy worrying about how to perform that he can't perform.

Another complicating factor is that many men with ADD/ADHD may not be motivated to change their behavior in this realm of life. When it comes to finding—or keeping—a job, the consequences of failing to change are more immediate. Getting fired is, after all, a pretty concrete thing.

However, when it comes to a couple's sex life, both partners may simply find ways to cope without sex, or put up with the situation for much longer periods of time. Consciously or unconsciously, many husbands with ADD/ADHD understand this dynamic, which allows them to justify their behavior or attitude toward sex and avoid making changes.

Blogger Bryan Hutchinson (adderworld.com) writes about the challenges of living with ADD/ADHD in a non-ADD/ADHD world. His thoughts on sex may prove enlightening to wives whose husbands lack the words to explain their thought processes:

[To a man with ADD], sex is boring. We'd rather be doing something else while in the act of having sex, something more exciting, like, well, fantasizing about sex . . . Physical sex is unsatisfying because it never seems to live up to our expectations . . .Too many of us continue to create and build on a fantasy no one person can ever hope to fulfill. Porn will never fill the void... it's like a like a chocolate craving, the last bite is never enough, because it isn't quite as satisfying as one had hoped. And yet, the hunger for more chocolate continues. There is no last bite of chocolate.

In essence, when one of the sex partners has ADD/ADHD, what happens in the bedroom is a microcosm of the rest of life. Whatever symptoms a wife sees in her husband in the outside world are likely to be magnified and amplified in the bedroom.

Nevertheless, there is hope. For starters, looking for excuses or blaming each other won't help. Rather, it is imperative that you both get on the same page. If, as the wife, you have things you want to share with your husband, try not to vent to him about it. Whether or not they deserve it, men tend to turn off when they feel they are being yelled at, insulted or blamed. This will close down the pathways of communication between you two and likely devolve into a fight.

Instead, vent your frustrations about your husband to a professional counselor or a trusted friend. Then, when you're ready to talk to your husband, communicate your needs in ways that seek his help, rather than blaming him for the problem (even if you see it as his fault). A productive strategy is to gently but firmly encourage him to state his problem and enlist your assistance in solving it. The following ideas may help the two of you rekindle the spark:

Put romance on the calendar: Sometimes adding a romantic interlude to a busy to-do list is just what the doctor ordered. Seeing sex on a list of so many other things to do in a given day may grab his interest by working with his ADD/ADHD symptoms. Your date ends up being a welcome distraction from all the other things on his mind, rather than the other way around.

Deal with distractions: This may take different forms for different people. In some cases, the husband with ADD/ADHD cannot deal with a quiet room—mostly because those rooms are never quiet. There is always something creaking, murmuring, or buzzing in the background. For men with ADD/ADHD, these distractions are sure-fire libido killers. If that is the case, make sure all of these potential distractions have been dealt with beforehand. At the same time, some men with ADD/ADHD prefer some kind of "white noise" in the background, whether it's a television or radio playing in a non-intrusive way.

Go for variety: Change the duration of your encounters. As the wife, you may want to arouse his interest by surprising him with a quick, sexy kiss or by dropping an item of clothing just when he is doing something else. This applies to foreplay as well. Not every sexual encounter has to end with intercourse. Wives may want to adopt a playful "shock and awe" strategy for a while, in which their husbands never know what they will be hit with sexually.

Recapture respect: It's often been said that "the brain is the most important sex organ." Many wives find themselves losing respect for their ADD husbands as time goes by. This directly affects the couple's sex life. To help reverse this trend, begin to identify those things you admire about your husband and encourage him to do more of them. For example, if you love the way he hangs pictures in the house, turn your hallways into art galleries! If you love the way he fixes your car, have him change the oil—frequently and in your presence! Respect for your husband can be a powerful aphrodisiac—make him get out there and earn it!

[9]

Little Boy Syndrome

I n the beginning, he was cute, funny and a total riot. Many women fondly recall their courtship with their ADD/ADHD husband as something out of a fairy tale. Others were simply taken by his child-like qualities. Years later, however, the very qualities that first swept you off your feet now seem anything but cute and endearing. Instead, they seem like the tip of an iceberg of other problems caused by his ADD/ADHD. Instead of being her husband's best friend and lover, she finds herself stuck in the role of mother, maid and taskmaster.

Welcome to the Little Boy Syndrome. Melissa R., an accountant living in Stamford, Connecticut, encapsulated how many wives of ADD/ADHD feel several years into their marriage, long after their husbands' "boyish charm" has worn off.

I feel like a single mom. He is an adult. I should not have to call and make sure he is on task several times a day as if he is a 12-year-old boy at home with a list of chores! I'm the one that cleans, does the dishes, does the laundry, buys the groceries, drives us everywhere, feeds the pets, and works 10-hour days.

Though it has not yet obtained an official diagnosis, the Little Boy Syndrome is extremely real to wives who live with it day after day. Some of the symptoms of this side effect of ADD/ADHD include the following:

Communication Problems: Men with ADD/ADHD often appear to live in an alternative universe. They may "zone out," talk out of turn, change the subject without warning, or simply ignore you. Sound like a four-year-old? You bet.

Trouble Completing Tasks: ADD/ADHD breeds awful organizational skills and forgetfulness. A man with ADD/ADHD may routinely forget important dates like birthdays or anniversaries. How's that as an aphrodisiac?

Inability to Take Responsibility: If you ask your ADD/ADHD husband to pay a bill, cut the grass, or make sure the toxic cleaner gets put away so the children can't get to it, you can almost always expect that it will not get done.

Lack of Impulse Control: Whether it's quitting a job without warning, buying an expensive "toy" on impulse, driving too fast when the kids are in the car, or a host of other childish actions, your ADD/ADHD husband has difficulty understanding the natural, likely consequences of impulsive behavior. It is all an outgrowth of his constant search for stimulation. This can also manifest itself in emotional outbursts or arguments that quickly spiral out of control. If your husband were a toddler, these episodes would be referred to as "tantrums." As an adult, they are more like nightmares—for you!

Hyperfocus Dating: Perhaps this should have been mentioned first. Many women who marry men with ADD/ADHD honestly do not know what happened to the guy they fell in love with. After all, when you were dating, he could not get enough of you. Now that you are married, his excitement seems to have dissipated. The truth is, you did nothing wrong. Hyperfocus dating is simply another facet of ADD/ADHD for men. Like a little boy, he saw you simply as the shiny new object of his desire.

Not surprisingly, this upsets many wives, who end up feeling like yesterday's newspaper. In an effort to spark the old flame, one woman considered changing her hairstyle every week to see if it would help. However, before you book a hair appointment, understand that your ADD/ADHD husband's failure to pay attention to you is another side effect of his condition.

Change rarely comes easily, but it is possible. The first rule? Don't act like his mother. Therapists who deal with ADD/ADHD couples will unequivocally tell you that the most destructive pattern you can fall into is to treat your husband like the little boy he appears to be. Yes, you may feel that if you don't take care of things, nothing will get done. Yes, you may see that he does not react unless you nag him (or even when you do nag him). However, parenting is for parents, not for spouses. If you remain his mother, one thing is guaranteed: he will never change, and you will go through life as the frustrated, nagging wife you promised yourself you would never become.

Once you have made this decision, it becomes much easier to address your situation by taking it out of the realm of feelings and emotions and putting it into the realm of solutions. A good strategy is to approach the problem from your husband's point of view. In many ways, yes, he suffers from Little Boy Syndrome; but, at the same time, he is still an adult. Consider the following strategies:

When making a request of your husband, touch him. People with ADD/ADHD tend to take in information via their senses. Tactile involvement helps concentration.

If you want to speak to him, make eye contact. If you talk to him from the other side of the room, it is harder for him to identify with you, and you may be overlooked. Go in with a plan. Look him in the eyes. Keep it short, sweet, and to the point.

Set a time limit, and remind him later. When making a request, let him know that you would appreciate it being fulfilled by a specific date or time. Ask for his commitment on that. Ask for permission to remind him frequently. When following through on the reminders, remind yourself to be pleasant.

Do not assume he will get to everything on your list, so break things down into smaller portions. When planning tasks or chores in your brain, assume things will take more time than you want them to. Be ready to adapt and reprioritize in midstream.

PART 3

SOLUTIONS FOR ADD/ADHD

[10]

Medication

Medication can be a very effective treatment for ADD/ADHD. Since ADD/ADHD is essentially a neurobiological disorder caused by a genetic chemical imbalance in the brain, medication helps restore the proper balance. Many husbands complain that they know what to do, but don't know how to get it done. Either they are prone to distraction or their brains seem locked in a haze. Thus far, studies indicate that medication is the best remedy for decreasing these and other symptoms associated with ADD/ADHD.

Dr. Dmitri Malkin, a psychiatrist who treats clients with ADD/ADHD in New York City, notes that "finding the right kind of medication is generally the easy part."

"The harder, and more important part, is finding the right kind of behavior modifications through therapy that help [people with ADD/ADHD] learn the skills they were never taught, so that they can function normally without the need for medication," he said.

Dr. Malkin explains that there two basic families of stimulant medication to treat ADD/ADHD: amphetamines and methylphenidates. Patients with certain symptoms receive methylphenidates (such as Focalin), because they need a way to calm their thoughts and concentrate on the task at hand. Other symptoms (remember—there are 18 symptoms in all) benefit from amphetamine drugs (like Adderall), which clear away the "fog."

Stimulants improve ADD/ADHD symptoms in roughly three-fourths of adults, and slightly higher percentages in children. They reduce hyperactive symptoms, including problems with focus, impulsive behavior, aggression, defiance, and task completion. In addition, stimulant medication can greatly increase concentration, work productivity, emotional control, and appropriate social behavior.

Stimulants are one the most researched medications in psychiatry, having been in use for more than 40 years, with over 400 studies over thousands of cases. The delivery system of the medication, e.g., short/long acting, immediate acting, etc., has been steadily improving, making the medications even more effective as the science advances. The short-acting forms of the drug are usually taken two or three times per day and the long-acting type only once per day.

Stimulants are not considered to be habit-forming, because the doses used are too small to produce narcotic-like dependency. However, there is a slight potential for abuse or addiction with any stimulant medication, especially if a person has a history of substance abuse or addiction. Common side effects include headache, decreased appetite, insomnia, upset stomach, and elevated blood-pressure. The major side effects last only a few weeks while the body gets used to the new medication.

Only a psychiatrist can determine which medication is right for your husband, and often he or she will prescribe multiple medications at once to see which work the best. Since the medication starts to take affect quickly, many psychiatrists will encourage their patients to try a few different brands before deciding which one produces the best results. The degree of improvement with ADD/ADHD medication is significantly greater than for many other psychiatric drugs, which means there is hope for improving your husband's symptoms, even though there is no "cure" for the disorder.

[11]

Diet & Exercise

Many of today's diets focus on "getting skinny quickly," without helping people achieve lasting results. However, adopting a diet of balanced meals will do wonders for your husband's emotional balance. Many dieticians recommend the 40/40/20 rule. This means daily intake should include (approximately) 40 percent protein (meat, fish, eggs, beans), 40 percent carbohydrates (breads, fruits, vegetables), and 20 percent fats (olive oil, peanut oil, avocados, nuts, soy, tofu).

We recommend following the Zone Diet by Dr. Sears. Originally designed for athletes to maintain peak conditioning, the Zone Diet is effective at reducing glucose spikes, which seem to negatively impact ADD/ADHD symptoms.

Sugar

Food plays a huge role in the way we feel emotionally and physically. The chemicals in our brain respond differently to different food chemicals, resulting in varying effects on our behavior. As such, it is important to identify the few foods that have the most effect on your husband's ADD/ADHD.

Men with ADD/ADHD commonly eat large amounts of sugar in various forms on a daily basis. Some people eat jelly beans constantly; others pour packets of sugar into their morning coffee. Generally, if sugar is an important element in your husband's daily food intake, there's a reason. Most Americans are addicted to sugar (this mean they will feel at least minor withdrawal symptoms for several days if sugar were removed completely from their diet). Beyond that, however, people with ADD/ADHD use sugar as a drug to self-medicate the affects their condition has on their brain. In most cases, they remain unaware why they need the sugar. Rather, they just know it "works."

ADD/ADHD inhibits the communication between the front (actions) and back (thoughts) parts of your husband's brain. Medication removes the barrier between the two parts and helps them function more smoothly together. Sugar also acts as a lubricant between the front and back parts of your husband's brain, allowing him to more successfully put his thoughts into action. The fact that sugar is so effective in alleviating the symptoms of adult ADD/ADHD is the reason so many people with the disorder find themselves constantly consuming the substance. Unfortunately, consuming too much sugar brings its own side effects.

For example, high sugar-intake can be the cause of moodiness in many people with ADD/ADHD. However, sugar often goes undetected as the culprit, because most foods contain sugar as an additive. Everything from bread to vegetable broth—and just about everything in between—contains sugar these days. So while eating sugar enhances your husband's energy level and mood for a short time, he may become extremely moody after the effects of the sugar have worn off several hours later.

Ideally, your husband will change his diet to remove all foods that are high in refined sugar. Refined sugars are those sugars that do not naturally appear in food. For example, an apple has sugar in it, but that sugar is natural to the apple; it has no refined sugars in it. We need sugars to survive, and are supposed to eat several fruits and vegetables every day for this very reason. But removing as much refined sugar from your husband's diet as possible will greatly benefit his health and mood.

The following list, comprised with help from dietician Namita Nayyar, details the top five foods for your husband to avoid:

White Flour

All the good substances (bran and germ) are removed from flour during processing. White flour makes blood sugar rise almost as much as refined sugar. Intestinal infections are a direct outcome of white flour consumption. Foods made from white flour have no nutritional value and may cause more harm than good to your husband's body. Combine white flour, refined sugar and high heat baking and you have the perfect combination to aggravate his ADD/ADHD symptoms.

Soda

The human body should take in no more than 40 grams of sugar every day. One raw apple has 15 grams of natural sugar. One can of regular Coke has 39 grams of refined sugar. It also contains 150 empty calories, 50 mg of caffeine, and a ton of harmful artificial food colors, flavorings, and preservatives—all of which have zero nutritional value. Some soda drinks labeled as "diet soda" contain dangerous sweeteners like aspartame. Numerous health side effects are associated with aspartame ingestion, including brain damage, diabetes, emotional disorders, decreased vision, ringing in the ears, memory loss, heart palpitations, shortness of breath, and more.

Meal Replacement Bars

In this fast-paced world, energy and meal replacement bars might seem like an easy way to pack in some important vitamins and minerals while giving a little lift. Sure, they have more nutritional value than a candy bar, but most also have just as many calories and just as much sugar as those same candy bars. The high sugar content causes a sugar rush and then crash, leaving your husband moody and hungry for more. Some bars with alcohol sugars do help avoid such a crash. Check the labels.

Breakfast Cereals

Many common breakfast cereals are packed with simple sugars that might start your husband's day with a jolt, but lead to trouble down the line. A typical cereal in this country today has around 15 grams of sugar per serving, while only providing 1 gram of dietary fiber and 2 grams of protein. These cereals end up being empty calories.

Ice Cream – Candy - Cookies

These yummy treats are basically empty calories, full of sugar while providing little benefit, but most of them contain those awful trans fats. Once in a while will not make a great difference, but if your husband is eating them with any regularity, his ADD/ADHD will be severely impacted. The sugar content may exceed the 50 grams of sugar mark for only one serving of candy or ice cream. And eating sugar at night, in the form of dessert, is most likely contributing to your husband's surge in energy around midnight, causing him to stay up until all hours of the night.

Water

Most people fail to drink enough water. Believe it or not, men should drink about 3 liters a day, and women should drink 2.2 liters a day. This means that unless your husband makes a concerted effort to drink water throughout the day, he is not drinking enough. Why is water more important for a man with ADD/ADHD? The answer lies in the fact that the brain is 80 percent water.

ADD/ADHD is a neurological disorder. If your husband's brain is operating on insufficient amounts of water, it won't function properly. Problems with focus are most often the ones alleviated by proper hydration.

You are most likely to be successful in changing your husband's water-drinking habits if you show that you are willing to change with him. Regardless of whether or not you yourself are getting enough water every day, use the following suggestion to get your husband on track to drink enough water daily. During your next trip to the grocery store, purchase a gallon jug of natural spring water for your husband and a 2-liter bottle for yourself. With both containers in hand, challenge your husband to a drinking contest to see if you both can finish your water by the end of the day. Reuse the containers and challenge him again the next day, either to dethrone you as the first day's champion, or retain his title for another day. After a few weeks of this, you both will be drinking the right amount of water daily.

Fish Oils

Omega-3 fatty acids have entered the public consciousness because of their potent health benefits. Most over-the-counter fish oil supplements are similar to each other. Stronger versions require a prescription. Physically, fish oils generally improve circulation, lowering the risk of a heart attack, and lower the cholesterol count. For people with ADD/ADHD, fish oils improve brain function, lubricating the necessary parts of the brain to help reduce ADD/ADHD symptoms.

Remember, the recommendations made in this book are intended to help reduce, rather than completely cure, your husband's ADD/ADHD symptoms. Like diabetes, the disorder never goes away. However, regular intake of measured doses of fish oils is one small, yet effective, way to help create the best possible environment for your husband's brain.

Exercise

For men with ADD/ADHD, exercise poses less of a problem. Since most of these men feel lots of energy most of the time, they may have already spent their childhood playing sports. As adults, they continue to find athletics a source of stress relief. Some types (ADD/ADHD—Inattentive) may never have been very active. These men need more assistance getting started on an exercise plan. However, there is no lack of effective exercise programs available online, which offer a disciplined exercise regimen in the home. These programs will improve your husband's chances of sticking with a challenging program in part because they save him the task of figuring out how he is going to fit exercise into his day.

[12]

Doing His "Work"

I n this context, "Work" happens when someone addresses his or her own psychological and emotional problems head-on. For example, you are reading this book to improve your quality of life and deal with the problems surrounding your husband's ADD/ADHD. And while the information presented may be helpful to you, processing through it requires a certain level of psychological and emotional vulnerability and pain. So just by reading this book, YOU are doing YOUR "Work."

One of the best places your husband can go to do his "Work" is in the therapist's office. Therapy for ADD/ADHD focuses on the most aggravated symptoms the client exhibits and teaches him how to manage those symptoms more effectively. As stated before, there is no 100 percent cure for ADD/ADHD. Medication can greatly reduce symptoms, but like diabetes, ADD/ADHD must be consistently managed throughout a person's life.

While many men with ADD/ADHD may deny they have it or resist going for a diagnosis, others find that gaining a deeper understanding of their disorder brings them a measure of relief. "I've struggled with ADD/ADHD all my life," said Stan D., a computer programmer who lives in suburban Boston. "It went undiagnosed in my childhood, because I was intelligent and people weren't very aware of this disorder in the '80s. There were definite signs of it though, and it's affected my life to this day.

As an example of the challenges he has faced, Stan noted that he failed to graduate high school on time and was unable to "complete a college degree and get a real job" throughout his twenties.

Until that point, my life had been all about wasted potential. Thankfully, I sought treatment a few years ago, and through therapy and medication, I have been able to straighten up my life a bit. I'm engaged to a great girl, and I will be graduating this year, a little before my 30th birthday.

Not all therapies are created equal. Make sure you choose a therapeutic approach that will yield the results you are both looking for. Beth S., a special education teacher in Los Angeles, learned this the hard way.

My former husband and I did all sorts of talk therapy, and it accomplished nothing. Talking a person with ADD/ADHD into paying attention is like politely asking a diabetic to make more insulin. Not going to happen.

What, then, are the hallmarks of effective therapy for men with ADD/AHDD? While each patient is different, most will benefit from these basic techniques:

Changing habits: ADD/ADHD therapy helps people identify specific problematic behaviors and change them. A good therapist will help your husband learn ways to manage himself. For example, rewards can be proposed as an incentive to complete specific tasks, such as playing that favorite game on his phone after answering his boss's emails.

Getting organized: Effective ADD/ADHD therapy focuses on various ways to reduce the chaos. People with this disorder need visual and auditory cues to remember things. Learning to incorporate tools—ranging from Post-it notes to iCal—will help them function better. A good therapist will have very specific recommendations, right down to how your husband can best organize his closet. That level of specificity can be a huge help with adult ADD/ADHD.

Repairing relationships: As you know, adult ADD/ADHD affects more than just the person with the diagnosis. It also affects you, your children, and the extended family as well. As such, some elements of ADD/ADHD therapy may include other family members. On the one hand, it can help them better understand your husband's disorder. On the other hand, it may provide a safe place to rid themselves of a lot of anger that they had to swallow before the diagnosis.

Challenging negative beliefs: Over the years, men with ADD/ADHD tend to accumulate a lot of self-doubt. They come to think that many tasks are beyond them and give up. Therapy can help them question these self-limiting beliefs and overcome them.

Improving social skills: Men with ADD/ADHD often lack important social skills. They might have poor communication or a tendency to interrupt when someone else is talking. Therapy can help them learn how to pick up on social cues and interact with people better. Eventually, they will feel more comfortable in social settings and can overcome their difficulties in interacting with others.

Treating other conditions: There is a 4-in-10 chance that a man with ADD/ADHD also suffers from another psychiatric condition, such as anxiety or depression. Those conditions alone often require therapy. All the more so when grouped with ADD/ADHD.

Therapy is more than just two people talking. Unlike a friend or relative, the therapist creates a secure environment in which the client feels safe sharing his most personal thoughts and feelings. The therapist is also the client's ally, supporting him unconditionally in achieving his goals and at all times keeping in view the best interests of the client. Numerous scientific studies have proven that the therapeutic relationship itself is transformational in improving the client's well-being, simply because it gives the client an outlet to air his problems and a safe place to feel accepted, validated, and understood. Unlike friends and relatives, therapists are trained professionals who help shed light on aspects of the client's thoughts and feelings that the client may not be able to see on his own.

However, therapy will not work for your husband unless he is a willing and cooperative client. It will be helpful if you explain your concern from a loving perspective with the intention of simply suggesting that he give this a try.

After he has agreed to proceed, the first step is to get with a professional. That means a licensed social worker, psychologist or psychiatrist, who specializes in working with adult ADD/ADHD. The professional will need to understand how your husband functioned as a child, in school, social settings, and in personal relationships, in order to determine the proper therapeutic approach.

Men's Work

One of the best ways for men to get support while doing their "Work" is through Men's Work. In the past few decades, men's organizations have formed in record numbers in many countries around the world. One of the most respected is The ManKind Project (www.MKP.org), an international not-for-profit group of volunteer men who facilitate weekend retreats (New Warrior Training Adventures) to help men improve their EQ (Emotional Intelligence).

Organizations like The ManKind Project also have ongoing weekly support groups where men can openly share their struggles and successes, and get validation, support, and input from other members of the group. While the initial weekend retreats often cost money, most of the ongoing weekly group meetings are free. Some organizations, like author David Deida's men's circles (www.daviddeida.meetup.com), are completely free and require no prior commitment to attend. Encourage your husband to attend and participate in a men's group; it will undoubtedly be a positive experience for him.

Sometimes one of the greatest fears a wife faces is the fear that her husband will change how he feels about her once he becomes more attuned to himself and his identity. In most cases, simply talking about your fears alleviates many concerns. Generally, a man will take MORE responsibility for the health of the relationship once he learns more about himself, his priorities, and how to live with greater integrity.

Men's Work is a gift for any man to experience. It is an opportunity for him to connect to his masculinity in a mature and healthy way, with the support of other men. For a variety of reasons, many men today fear other men, and even fear being a man themselves. Men's Work provides a safe space for a man to practice being the man he wants to be in a loving and supportive masculine environment. Men need to be in connection with other men. There is an aspect of healing and support that only other men can offer.

No matter how hard you try, women cannot offer men everything they need. Getting the rest of their needs met by other men is essential to healthy masculinity. Joining a men's group can help your husband better deal with his issues of ADD/ADHD and with the multitude of problems often associated with it.

[13]

Sleep Hygiene

I s your husband the type who sits down at his computer at 10:30 p.m. to start surfing the web? Or decides to engage in a massive spring cleaning right before bed? Or claims to be a night owl who is just getting started when the sun goes down? These are all common traits for adults with ADD/ADHD.

Getting a good night's sleep aids proper functioning in all adults, but especially in adults with ADD/ADHD. Recent science has evolved our understanding of sleep, putting the goal at approximately eight hours per night, but also acknowledging that any amount of uninterrupted sleep helps, such as a nap or waking up in the night but going back to sleep.

In his 2012 *New York Times* article, David Randall explains that "a number of recent studies suggest that any deep sleep—whether in an eight-hour block or a thirty-minute nap—primes our brains to function at a higher level, letting us come up with better ideas, find solutions to puzzles more quickly, identify patterns faster and recall information more accurately. In a NASA-financed study, for example, a team of researchers led by David F. Dinges, a professor at the University of Pennsylvania, found that letting subjects nap for as little as 24 minutes improved their cognitive performance."

Despite these benefits, many adults with ADD/ADHD have not had a good night's sleep in decades. One of the challenges standing in the way of proper sleep hygiene is that many adults with ADD/ADHD actually enjoy the energy boost they receive in the evenings before bed. Some claim that they get their best work done at this time of day. The downside, of course, is that they don't make it to bed until sometime between 1 a.m. and 3 a.m. When the rest of the world wakes up at 7 a.m., they find themselves forced to function on just a few hours of restless sleep.

Poor sleep hygiene harms your relationship with your husband in other ways as well. Operating on different sleep cycles limits the quality of physical contact that a couple needs to maintain intimacy. In addition, since your husband is perpetually "off schedule," he often lacks the energy to play with his children during the day.

One trick to better sleep is to start thinking about going to bed earlier. Just thinking about this will help your husband realize that the time for going to bed is a choice. He then needs to recognize that his brain cannot be relied upon to tell him when his body is tired, because it is too busy processing information. To counteract this, he needs to train himself to get better at looking at the clock and begin his "wind-down" time at the right time, regardless of how tired he feels.

Your husband may complain that it takes him a long time to wind-down. Even so, this does not require him to stay up until all hours every night. If his winding-down process takes three hours, then he should start that process at 9 p.m. with no excuses!

Research shows that close proximity to a bright computer screen or cell phone screen activates the pineal gland, which controls the amount of Melatonin in your body. Melatonin influences biological rhythms, including sleep. Staring at a computer or cell phone for hours before bed fools the brain into thinking it is time to wake up, as if the sun is shining brightly, and you should be ready for the day. Problem is, in the real world, it is bedtime.

If your ADD/ADHD husband can successfully limit distractions after 9:30 p.m., particularly cell phones and computer usage, he is halfway there. This step may take some practice, but in time new habits can form. So what should he do instead of surfing the Drudge Report or Facebooking friends at 10:30? Suggest a hot shower. Hot showers can do wonders to reduce the tension that builds up throughout the day and minimize the hyperactivity at night. Another alternative is to purchase an inexpensive electronic shoulder massager and encourage him to use it for 10 minutes each night to help him relax his way towards an appropriate bedtime.

Being mentally prepared for bed starting at 9:30 p.m., reducing distractions (particularly computers and cell phones), taking a hot shower, using a massager, and cuddling with a loved one can do one wonders to realign your husband's sleep cycle.

[14]

Empathy through Education

Education helps mitigate the symptoms of adult ADD/ADHD because it separates the reality of the disorder from the myths. By learning the truth about ADD/ADHD and how it works, you and your husband will no longer operate under the false truths about his abilities and deficiencies. By understanding that his condition is a brain-chemistry deficiency rather than a reflection of a neglectful childhood, a defect in personality or a character flaw, people with ADD/ADHD often find great relief and increased motivation to learn how to manage their symptoms.

This is the only book you will need to understand and navigate through the issues surrounding your husband's ADD/ADHD. However, as we stated up front, this book was written with you in mind, not your husband. He, on the other hand, will benefit from reading books written especially for people with ADD/ADHD. The best book we have found for men with ADD is *Taking Charge of Your ADD*, by Dr. Russell Barkley.

Written for people with ADD/ADHD, the book is broken down into smaller chapters and blurbs of information. In fact, your husband may be surprised that he is actually able to finish it. Most people with ADD/ADHD pick up a book and set it down again soon, with the intention of reading the rest. Since task completion remains a challenge, the book ends up being ignored. By writing a book about ADD for people with ADD/ADHD, taking into account their propensity for not completing tasks, Dr. Barkley has enabled such people to learn about all aspects of their disorder and has given them hope that they will be able to better manage their condition over the course of their lifetime.

Support Groups

Support groups are an excellent resource for you and your husband to learn about ADD/ADHD and deal with its impact on your lives. Most cities feature some sort of ADD/ADHD support group now. The structure of the meeting may vary from one location to another, but will typically provide time for you and your husband to share with the group your personal story. You, in turn, will be able to hear the stories of others and how they manage their ADD/ADHD.

After the meeting, attendees typically congregate at a local restaurant for further discussion and fellowship. There is no obligation to continue with the group, and typically no membership fees are charged. Some meetings ask for donations of around $5 to help meet the cost of renting the meeting space, but otherwise money is not a factor in one's ability to attend.

Attending these meetings is an invaluable experience. Hearing the stories of others with ADD/ADHD, and how they manage their disorder can have a galvanizing effect on you and your husband (yes, spouses are welcome to attend). These meetings give hope that living with this condition can be accomplished with grace. Numerous scientific studies have proven the positive effect of support groups, and the downside risk is minimal.

To find more information on ADD Support Groups, search the Internet in your area, or visit these examples: http://www.maaddsg.org or http://www.meetup.com/Adult-ADD-Support-Group-Manhattan/

Webinars are also a great resource for education and management of ADD/ADHD. The Attention Deficit Disorder Association (http://www.add.org) offers webinars and a host of other resources.

Attending a webinar or support group and reading about ADD/ADHD will help you and your husband understand his situation and how it can be managed to effectively reduce his symptoms. By understanding what his ADD/ADHD entails and what he can do to get support, you will develop a deeper sense of compassion for what he has been living with, and be the best partner you can be.

[15]

Nagging

To be sure, the wives of men with ADD/ADHD put up with a lot on a daily basis. In the name of fairness, however, we would be remiss if we neglected to mention at least a portion of his side of the story. From the husband's point of view, nagging never helps. In fact, too much nagging actually reinforces the very problem the wife wants to solve by her nagging. In a typical situation, the wife resents feeling like she has to be her husband's mother, and the husband resents being treated like a little boy. But that is exactly what both sides feel when communication devolves into nagging. Most people intuitively recognize this truth. The problem is that when emotions run high, it can be difficult to step back and adopt a more effective tone with each other.

Therefore, the next time you find yourself slipping into the nagging mode, try one or more of the following suggestions to get what you want from your husband:

Manage Your Expectations: Make sure you are asking for something that is realistic and appropriate. Does that light bulb need to be changed immediately?

Ask to Have Your Needs Met: Use "I" statements, not "you" statements. Say, "I feel much calmer when the Visa bill is paid on time," instead of, "you never pay the bill on time."

Set a Timeframe: Ask when your partner can expect to finish the task. ("Can you change the car oil this weekend?") Let him tell you when it works best for him to do it.

Alternative Solutions: Sometimes, it is worth it to hire a handyman, rather than harming your relationship by arguing.

Take a Breath: Recognize the pattern you are in and talk about how to address it as a team. You will both need to change your behavior. Setting new ground rules you both can live with will help.

Make Tasks More Fun: People with ADD/ADHD hate menial tasks, especially when they find them uninteresting. If you can find a way to make your requests for his help more fun for him, he will be more likely to do them without complaint. For example, if you need him to clean out the bathtub drain, instead of asking him repeatedly to fix it, write him a Post-it note similar to the following.

Dear Man of the House,

I am filled with hair and gunk. I wish I could be free of these things like I was in the good old days. Will you clean me out and relieve my discomfort?

--- Your Faithful Bathtub Drain

Yes, it may sound silly. But tools like this one will significantly cut down on the nagging cycle and motivate him better to complete the tasks you need from him. Removing the chance of a face-to-face confrontation about cleaning the drain will help your husband feel less threatened. Once he feels free from the possibility of being shamed by you, the pressure he normally feels to accomplish a task will diminish.

[16]

Staying Positive

As we spoke about in chapter six, it is not uncommon for people with ADD/ADHD to dip into periods of depression, especially before, and shortly after, being diagnosed with the disorder. Staying positive is important to all individuals, but it is particularly crucial for the wife of someone with ADD/ADHD. Even though you have been dealt a challenging hand, staying positive helps mitigate the conflict and confusion you both experience in your daily life together. Allowing yourself to become depressed will only add an additional burden to your already difficult situation.

Caryn G. is the director of Human Resources at a major health care company in the Midwest. In her professional work, she enjoys the fact that she can implement rules and regulations and keep things running smoothly. At home, however, chaos often reins, leaving her feeling particularly vulnerable to slipping into negative thoughts.

You're dealing with something ultimately which you have no control or say over. However you slice it, that's depressing. Management does not mean the condition is gone. There are days when the symp-

toms get the better of my husband and guess what—I go down with him.

Other women develop coping mechanisms that allow them to weather the inevitable down days by focusing on the larger picture. Hana M., an administrative assistant in Roanoke, Virginia, decided she needed to separate her thoughts about her situation from her husband's actual condition.

Staying positive is something I find very challenging as it requires a constant mental effort. I try to not let ADD/ADHD take center stage in my life. Really, it's his problem, but it can seem like the biggest thing in my life!

She explained that her husband's inability to focus "puts a big spotlight" on the ADD/ADHD behavior, which causes her to get caught up in his problems unnecessarily.

I start focusing and thinking about his behaviors or circumstances over and over again and again, as if I could make some sense of it. Instead, I have learned to prioritize what is really important. If it's not in the top three, whatever!

She went on to point out that she stops herself from "ruminating" with "prayer, music, or some other indulgence that improves the quality of my life."

I have to be sure that his ADD/ADHD is not the focus of my life, and it can take a lot of effort.

Taking a hint from Hana, there are strategies the wives of men with ADD/ADHD can adopt to improve not only the atmosphere in the home but also their own state of mind:

Laughter

More than a clever aphorism, the notion of increasing laughter really is the best medicine. Laughter is nature's way of providing free happy pills to improve positive feelings. At the hormonal level, increased laughter reduces stress. Laughter signals the release of endorphins in the brain, which causes a "feel-good" effect throughout the body. As a result, you feel upbeat, optimistic, and confident to overcome any difficulties in life. Even "fake" laughter counts. Simply moving your face muscles to mimic laughter, releases endorphins, causing increased happy feelings. So while "fake" laughter may sound insincere, it still triggers the same effect in your brain that real laughter does, thus producing the desired increase in feelings of positivity. Find ways to laugh for real, or use "fake" laughter when those things are available, and both you and your husband will find the increased positivity you can invite into your lives. Best of all, it can be done anytime and anywhere!

Gratitude

Appreciating what you have in life adds a powerful, and underrated, contribution to overall health. When you stop and take the time to reflect on all the positive things you already have in life, you benefit in two ways. First, you act positively by acknowledging the good things you have in life. The list may be short at first, but the more gratitude you show for what you already have, the more space you create to allow in more goodness. Over time, this erases negativity and replaces it with positive feelings.

Second, gratitude helps you acknowledge the present moment, the here and now, which is beneficial for staying positive. Constantly worrying about the future is stressful. By staying in the present, by being grateful as often as possible, you can improve your quality of life and positive feelings. In practice, writing down just a few things you are thankful for each night before going to bed will help you de-stress before sleep, giving you more restful sleep and a positive outlook when you wake up.

Nature

The power of nature is significant, and can greatly increase positive feelings, simply by being in its presence. Buy plants for your home. Take walks. Spend time outdoors. Getting away from honking cars, polluted air, and flashing lights, helps anyone to cope with daily stressors more efficiently. Nature is especially important for your ADD/ADHD husband, because it offers a whole new menu of objects to focus on. By retreating to nature, even if it's a walk through the park or a picnic by the field, negative symptoms of ADD/ADHD can be significantly reduced. So take your husband by the hand and grab some fresh air!

[17]

Organization

Organizational skills are a vital component of a happy and successful life. For the man with ADD/ADHD the idea of bringing organization to his distracted life may seem like an unattainable goal. Some men find that their time management, forgetfulness, and shifting focus, along with all of the other symptoms associated with this disorder, combine to create a toxic brew of chaos. Others refuse to get started because they fear that unless they achieve perfection their efforts are a waste of time. Still others lack the capacity to handle tasks like paying bills or filing important papers.

Bill F. is a rental car agent in San Jose, California. His inability to keep papers in order consistently causes friction with his wife. To be fair, he admits that organization is a "huge challenge" for him. Nevertheless, knowing that he has a problem has done little to improve his habits.

On my desk is a pile of mail and books in utter chaos. These piles extend out from the desk along the floor in a couple of directions. I once found a year-old paycheck under the pile there. I've lost or misplaced paychecks or failed to remember it was payday numerous times over the years.

While finding money might be a pleasant side effect of having ADD/ADHD, losing the right to drive is something else altogether.

I once failed to see notices saying my auto insurance had expired and eventually opened a piece of mail from the DMV saying my registration had been suspended for six months, and I had to turn in my plates. Yes, after that I got very used to taking the bus.

But Bill knew he needed to do something drastic to change his situation when his organizational challenges almost landed him in jail.

Another time I overlooked a jury summons, only to finally open a piece of mail saying that if I didn't show up, I could either be locked up for 30 days or pay a $10,000 fine. I answered the summons the next day.

One anonymous woman could easily be Bill's wife. In the course of working with a therapist, she took notes on what a "typical Saturday" with her husband looks like in her world, which she shared on a forum connected to additudemag.com. This is what she wrote:

It seems like every day with my ADHD hubby is crazy. This was Saturday: Cracked the screen on his iPhone. Do not ask me how many iPhones he has had. You don't want to know. Let the dogs out in the backyard; They ran away and he had to chase them all over the neighborhood. Told me he found the hole in the fence and "fixed" it. While he was out, I let the dogs out. They ran away, and I spent 30 minutes chasing them all over the neighborhood. Turns out 'fixing' the hole in the fence was just putting a trash can in front of it. He gets home and 'fixes' the hole. Let's the dogs out without watching them. Dogs run away. I lose my mind, and he finally checks the perimeter of the fence and fixes it properly with me watching. He buys expensive beer and puts it in the freezer to chill. He forgets about it and all the beer is frozen solid. While I am removing the frozen beer from the fridge, I see a suspicious bag. There is a bag of garbage in my freezer. Why? Who knows? I go in our bedroom and cry. He slams the back door and sits in the backyard stewing. Later, he asks me why I am never happy. This is every day. Every day. Not the same incidents, but equally crazy. He loses his keys to the house. He leaves all the windows down in the car and there is a torrential downpour. He turns the ringer off on his phone and no one can reach him all day. He loses the keys to his art studio and breaks a window to get in. He forgets to pay his credit card bill... again. He puts the ice cream in the refrigerator instead of the freezer. He starts the laundry and leaves it in the washer wet overnight.

If these words ring true, then you are no stranger to the daily frustration of living with a disorganized spouse and often have no clue how to improve the situation, short of giving up. Luckily, there are steps you can take if your husband's lack of organizational skills is driving you crazy:

Keep To-Do Lists Limited: Asking your husband to deal with an endless list will cause him to jump from one task to another without finishing anything. Instead, limit your to-do lists to no more than five tasks at a time. Once those five tasks are finished, start a new list. Both of you will feel more productive, less overwhelmed, and better able to manage your time. Worried you will forget something if you do not write it down? If it is really important, you will remember the task and can add it to your next list once your current list is finished.

Reward Yourselves: Making the transition from a disorganized family to an organized family does not happen overnight. This can be a big challenge for men with ADD/ADHD, because they lose interest quickly and are likely to leave you hanging if they don't have positive reinforcement to keep moving forward. To avoid pitfalls, set up a reward system to keep both you and your husband motivated. For example, every day you wash the dishes after dinner, instead of letting them sit in the sink for days, you earn a point. Once ten points are earned, you can treat each other to something you both enjoy—a basketball game or concert, or that fancy night out you reserve for special occasions.

Set Deadlines: Stop letting your husband spend days agonizing over decisions. Set a time and date by which to make your decisions and stick to that deadline. Remember, there is no "perfect" choice when tough decisions need to be made. And endless pro/con lists only further complicate the decision-making process. Make the best choice together and move on.

One Step at a Time: Help your husband break big projects into smaller, achievable steps. For example, if he is facing an upcoming presentation at work, construct a roadmap of easy-to-complete steps, then schedule one or two tasks to be completed on each day leading up to the presentation. View the completion of each small step as a major success, and reward him in little ways along the path to stay motivated.

Schedule Everything: Successful organization requires good time management, which is often a major challenge for men with ADD/ADHD. The more he writes down in his daily planner, the better.

Encourage your husband to schedule his day the night before and set cell phone or computer alarm reminders before each appointment or responsibility.

De-clutter Your Keepsakes: Keepsakes serve as an emotional reminder of good times past, which is important. But holding on to every sentimental object will clutter your home in a hurry. Set aside an hour every Sunday to catalog a few of your keepsakes at a time by photographing them and scrapbooking the photo with a descriptive paragraph about why the item is important to you. Then donate the items to Goodwill or the Salvation Army each week. You will hold on to all the memories in your Memory Book, and rid yourself of the clutter.

Give Your Keys a Home: After you have begun to de-clutter, take your organization to the next level by assigning a special place for your most used items, such as keys, wallet, mail, etc. Your husband's days of searching for lost keys will be over if you designate a spot and place them without fail. This provides quick access to the most used, frequently used household items and saves the time and stress of searching for them just as you or husband are running out the door.

Streamline Your Finances: Pick a time and date each month when you and your husband can sit down to review information regarding your bank accounts, investments, and retirement plans. Switch to online banking and have access to your account information 24/7. You will also be able to deposit checks from home electronically, saving valuable time and energy. Use a single checking account if possible, allowing for easier access and management of your finances. Keep credit cards to a minimum, limiting your open credit accounts to no more than two or three.

Hire an ADD/ADHD Therapist or Coach: Few of us like asking for help, but sometimes the best way to organize ourselves is to elicit the help of a professional. Encouraging your husband to work with a therapist or organization coach will put an ally in your corner who can support you in becoming a more organized and successful couple. He or she will motivate him to stay on the path, while helping him develop skills to more effectively manage time, incorporate a structured schedule, and prioritize tasks. You will have to invest time and money, but, in return, you will find yourself feeling better about your relationship.

[18]

Healing Your Relationship

Elationships, by nature, are challenging. But when your husband has ADD/ADHD, it can feel like a never-ending, constant uphill battle. Your husband may not know it yet, but his intimacy issues, temper, and inattentiveness towards your feelings could all be deeply connected to his ADD/ADHD. Knowing this probably does not make it any easier for you, but at least it explains his behavior in some way, and opens up a treatment avenue to explore.

Not much is yet known about the extent to which adult ADD/ADHD affects marriages and other intimate relationships, as there have been few clinical studies on this topic. In 2003, researchers from McGill University in Montreal looked at the impact of ADD/ADHD on the psycho-social functioning of children and spouses of adults with the disorder. The study compared 33 families with an ADD/ADHD parent/spouse with a control group of 26 families. The results showed that family and marital functions were significantly impaired in the ADD/ADHD families compared to the control group. The study also found that children with an ADD/ADHD parent exhibited more psychosocial problems and more co-morbidity than found in the controls.

Most wives of husbands with ADD/ADHD would concur with the study's results. In addition to the normal challenges of creating a happy home, having a husband with ADD/ADHD brings an additional "presence" in the relationship, one that is never really welcome and never really goes away.

Terri S. is an ice-skating instructor in Milwaukee, Wisconsin. She does not consider herself naïve or overly romantic when it comes to relationships. As she describes it:

We love each other very much, but we have our problems, like any couple. What's difficult for me isn't so much that we have problems—that's inevitable— it's that so many of them go unresolved.

This inevitably leads her to keep many of her irritations bottled up inside.

I try to address things in ways that won't destroy our relationship. But even after we address them, things seem to revert back to the way they were. It's almost as though he forgets we ever had the conversation.

As time goes on, Terri finds herself watching helplessly as her husband repeatedly tells her he will work on things, only to go on without making any real effort.

It makes me worry that my only alternatives are being unhappy, or leaving him altogether.

Often, however, women like Terri do not leave their husbands. Instead, they stay and suffer, sometimes loudly, sometimes in silence, sometimes with the help of medication of their own. Their lives become completely bound up in their husband's disorder. They feel embarrassed, demoralized, or find that nobody else understands their situation. Others find themselves increasingly isolated, because their husband's behavior demands all their attention, discouraging activities that do not focus on the husband, the marriage, or the house.

Frankly, this is no way to go through life. Humans are social creatures. Your husband's ADD/ADHD should not override your personal or social needs. Do everything you can to cultivate friendships. Insist on time for your own social world, where you can participate in activities that nourish YOU. It's critical to your health, which is just as important as your husband's.

At the same time, even if you have started to meet your own needs more effectively, your marriage may be teetering on the brink of collapse. To be sure, many wives in this situation simply opt for divorce. However, others prefer to salvage their marriage rather than go through the pain and disruption of ending it. Others remain conflicted about the idea of divorce for many years, because they lack the tools necessary to save their marriage.

Shlomo Slatkin is the author of the book, *Is My Marriage Over: The Five Step Action Plan to Saving Your Marriage*. He recommends the following five steps to help turn around a failing marriage:

Commit: While it may appear obvious, the couples whose marriages do not survive are usually those not committed to making their marriages work. When you make the decision to commit, you have decided to put in the hard work that is needed to save your marriage. When you waver and think about what it would be like if you married someone else or how you wish your life would be different, you are usually not able to generate enough momentum to push forward and repair the relationship. When deciding whether or not to commit, be aware of the consequences divorce can have on your children and your finances. Also, realize that it takes two to tango, and that finding someone better is not necessarily a cure-all; the same or similar issues are likely to recur in future relationships. Finally, recognize how the particular challenges of your marriage are growth opportunities for you and your spouse, and that there are ways for you to transform this conflict into connection. (Of course, this does not apply to abusive relationships.)

Seal your exits: Couples in crisis are often focused everywhere but on their marriage. It's so painful, who can blame them? Even if they are legally still married, many of them have "checked out." An essential step to bringing the energy back into the relationship is to seal your exits. This means thinking about the various activities where you focus your inner resources, and deciding whether they have become substitutes for the excitement and fulfillment of marriage. Besides the obvious (often-fatal) exits of infidelity and substance abuse, here are a few of the more common exits that we may find ourselves engaging in:

- Work
- Exercise
- Overeating
- Facebook or other social media
- Taking care of the kids

While many of these activities may be harmless, if one of the reasons you are doing them is to avoid spending time with your spouse, it may only be an exit. Become aware of how you may be exiting the relationship, and begin to close those exits by putting more energy where it needs to be.

Detoxify your marriage: Eliminate the name-calling, finger-pointing, blaming, and shaming. A toxic relationship cannot thrive. Angry outbursts chip away at the love and trust that a couple has for each other. Instead, take ownership for your feelings and frustration by focusing on why your spouse's actions disturb you. Replace the "you" of "you always do this" with "I"—"how I felt when ..." Finally, learn to ask for what you want. It's so easy to complain that we often forget what it is we are missing. Rather than focusing on how your spouse ignores you, share how badly you crave his love and attention. Not only does detoxifying your marriage help to remove the poison from your relationship, it will make your spouse much more amenable to meeting your needs.

Enter the world of the other: One of the painful realizations that married people discover is that "my spouse is not me." In order to make room for the other, it is critical to learn to acknowledge that your spouse may see the world very differently than you. We do that by learning how to communicate more safely. When we talk, we want to connect and make sure that our spouse hears us. Get into the habit of asking, "Is now a good time?" instead of dumping a verbal assault. If the goal is to connect, make sure your spouse is mentally and emotionally available to connect. The second step occurs when we listen. Try to enter the other's world by listening and understanding without responding or interjecting. Although in your world, things may look entirely different, be curious and interested in what your partner is saying. You may be surprised at what you discover. Couples are so often caught up in their own world that is hard to make sense of the other's experience. In successful relationships, both partners are allowed to express their own feelings safely and work together to bridge the gap between their worlds.

Love infusions: Working on any relationship is challenging, especially so when you are trying to rescue someone in crisis. That's why it is crucial to infuse your relationship with loving behaviors that promote positive energy. These love infusions help lighten things and add fun:

By showing appreciation – The best way to decrease resentment and reinforce positive behavior is by expressing appreciations. When we share what we like about our spouse, we begin to focus on what is right in the relationship, and our partner feels that his efforts are valued. More than a simple thank you, sit down with your spouse, look into her eyes, tell her what you appreciate about her, and why it means so much to you. By spending a few minutes a day on this exercise, you can break through a lot of negativity.

Date night – Even if you've been married for 40 years, you still need to date your spouse. Make a set time once a week to go out together and enjoy each other's company. Whether that means going out for dinner or for a walk in the park, take this time to enjoy face-to-face connection. By making a fixed appointment, you will show each other that the marriage is a priority.

Caring behaviors – Love is a verb. We demonstrate care for a spouse when we perform loving behaviors. Every individual is different, so it is important to find out from your spouse what types of behaviors make him/her feel cared for. Ask him to write a list of behaviors that he particularly appreciates, and try to demonstrate one such caring behavior each day.

Final Thoughts

In an age of information overload, many people seeking help for their challenges—no matter what they may be—often find it exceedingly difficult to find help for their particular situation. Certainly this is the case with wives of ADD/ADHD husbands. As we began counseling clients with the disorder, it became painfully obvious that their chaotic life HAD to be affecting the significant people in their lives—especially their spouses. Yet, as we began to research the matter, other than a few scattered articles, we could not find a book dedicated to helping the non-ADD/ADHD partner cope with her situation. To us, this was a glaring oversight—bordering on negligence, to be honest—and we found ourselves in the position of having to take action.

That was the motivation behind the writing of this book. We readily admit that the information provided cannot substitute for peer-reviewed, clinical studies of the effects of adult ADD/ADHD on spouses and in particular, wives. However, we do hope that you will have found this to be a comprehensive treatment of the kinds of challenges you face every day, and that the tips and solutions recommended will put you on the path to a happier, healthier marriage with your husband. Though it requires work, every woman deserves a happy marriage with a partner she respects. Too often, the wife of a husband with ADD/ADHD faces her challenges alone. We hope this book represents a first step in helping you get the support that you need to do your own "Work," and helping your husband with the energy you have left. Remember: YOU come first!

Acknowledgments

The authors would like to thank the following supporters and collaborators who helped make this book a reality.

Dr. Russell Barkely

Rachel Fonseca

Steve & Julie Fonseca

Dr. Ned Hallowell

Bill & Paula Hurlbert

Dr. Kyle Lapidus

LaMar & Karen Norman

Andrew Norman

Lincoln Norman

Autumn Norman

Dr. Dmitri Malkin

David Ordan, senior copy editor, project manager

Dan & Ruth Sachs

Richard Sussman

About the Authors

George Sachs PsyD

Dr. Sachs is a licensed child and adult psychologist, specializing in the treatment of ADD/ADHD and Autism Spectrum Disorders in children, teen and adults. He is founder of the Sachs Center on the Upper West Side of Manhattan, serving individuals and families looking for answers to ADD/ADHD.

Dr. Sachs did his clinical training in Chicago at Cook County Hospital, Mt. Sinai Hospital and the Child Study Center. He completed his internship and post-doctoral work at the Children's Institute in Los Angeles, where he supervised and trained therapists in Trauma-Focused Cognitive Behavioral Therapy (TFCBT).

George Sachs is a Gestalt trained therapist, certified by the Gestalt Associates Training program of Los Angeles. Dr. Sachs consulted to Juilliard in New York City, providing counseling to their dance, drama, and orchestral students.

Dr. Sachs is the author of *The Mad Sad Happy Book*, a picture book that teaches emotional literacy to preschoolers. He also authored *Helping the Traumatized Child*, a workbook for traumatized children. Dr. Sachs has appeared on NBC Nightly News, CBS, WPIX, Vice TV and other major media outlets, discussing his unique holistic approach to ADD/ADHD treatment. Dr. Sachs also writes for the Huffington Post. Dr. Sachs is a member of the American Psychological Association and the New York State Psychological Association.

Tim Norman LCSW, M.Ed

Tim is a Licensed Clinical Social Worker and the Clinical Director of Neurofeedback at the Sachs Center. As a therapist, Tim has had success treating a variety of psychological and developmental issues, including: anxiety, attention/focus issues ADHD, depression, grief, PTSD, infidelity, relationships, and more.

At the Neurofeedback clinic, Tim has worked with a broad range of patients, from professional athletes and CEO's working on peak performance, to individuals and families with traditionally labeled psychological and medical disorders.

Timothy is a member of the International Society of Neurofeedback and Research (ISNR), the Association of Applied Psychophysiology and Biofeedback (AAPB), and the National Association for Social Workers (NASW).

He received his undergraduate degree (BA) from The Ohio State University, Master's in Education (MA) from Mercy College, and MSW from Hunter College School of Social Work. Timothy also serves on the Board of Directors for the Mankind Project International, a 401(c)(3) non-profit organization where he facilitates emotional literacy and leadership training for men of all ages.

SACHSCENTER

The Sachs Center is a full service boutique practice focused on the testing and treatment of ADD/ADHD and Aspergers in children, teens and adults. We go beyond labels, taking a holistic, person-centered approach to treatment.

We know how scary it can be when you are facing a problem in your life that you can't solve by yourself. For most of us, reaching out for help is not easy. Our approach to therapy centers around the belief that we need CONNECTION in order to heal. The relationship between the client and therapist IS the healing piece. From that connection, you will feel safe and empowered. Then, exploring your problems seems manageable and finding solutions becomes possible. Our office provides the comfort and confidentiality of a small private practice, with the breadth of services found in larger clinics.

George Sachs Psy.D.

Call Us: 646-807-8900
Text us: 646-418-5035
Email Us: george.sachs@sachscenter.com
Website: www.sachscenter.com

9 780996 950718